Popular Chinese Expressions

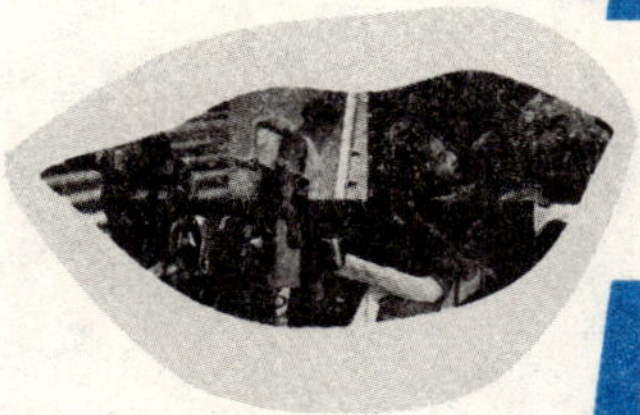

流行汉语

李淑娟 主编

华语教学出版社
SINOLINGUA

First Edition 2007

Second Printing 2008

ISBN 978-7-80200-388-0

Published by Sinolingua

24 Baiwanzhuang Road, Beijing 100037, China

Tel: (86)10-68320585

Fax: (86)10-68326333

http://www.sinolingua.com.cn

E-mail: hyjx@sinolingua.com.cn

Printed by Beijing Foreign Languages Printing House

Distributed by China International Book Trading Corporation

35 Chegongzhuang Xilu, P.O. Box 399

Beijing 100044, China

Printed in the People's Republic of China

Preface

The term "Catchwords" or "Catchphrases" refers to words and phrases which appear in a certain period or in a region, and are very popular. These words or phrases are mostly new words or adaptations of foreign words. Some words or phrases are old, but with new meanings; some are from unique dialects, slang or jargon. Therefore, catchwords have strong temporal and regional characteristics.

The usage of catchwords is very wide, covering all aspects of people's lives. Generally speaking, it includes both written and spoken language.

Catchwords as the most modern words and phrases are closely linked with the development and evolution of a society. In every period of time, many words and phrases are born reflecting social development. In recent years, as China has seen expanding reform and opening to the outside world, more new words and phrases have emerged and become wide spread. Today, the most popular catchwords are "ba rong ba chi", "he xie she hui", "ji min", "gu min", etc. These words all reflect elements of the time and society at large, as well as the course of societal development. However, because of the characteristics of time, catchwords come and go quickly. Some words or phrases gradually fade out and became nothing more than a memory.

This book, as a Chinese-English modern Chinese dictionary, includes the most popular words and phrases of the 21st century, especially those emerged in the past two years, including words and phrases frequently used in both the media and daily life. All entries are newly created and cover the fields of politics, society, economy, science and technology, culture and entertainment, fashion, Internet, work and study, and general life.

This book contains nearly 800 entries, and each entry includes stem, phonetic notation, definitions and examples. All stems are provided with phonetic notation and explained in English. For stems with more than one meaning, numerical notations are used to differentiate between alternate meanings. Each meaning of a word or phrase includes an example to clarify its usage. The book is arranged in alphabetic order. All words capitalized with western letters are listed at the back of the texts.

Along with the popularity of Chinese in countries outside China, more and more people have begun learning Chinese. In order to meet their needs, I have compiled this book especially for overseas students, Chinese abroad, foreigners who can speak Chinese, foreign scholars who study Chinese issues, and students at middle schools and universities outside China. The purpose of this book is to help those people to study and understand the meanings and expressions of the words or phrases they read in newspapers and magazines, watch on TV and hear in everyday conversations. As it is published in Chinese and English, it might also serve as a reference book for translators in China.

While compiling and translating this book, I have received great help and support from many friends. I wish to acknowledge my debt particularly to Mr. Han Jingti, Senior Research Fellow of the Institute of Linguistics of the Chinese Academy of Social Sciences, Vice-President and Secretary-General of China Lexicographical Association, who gave me useful guidance, and the editors and leaders of the publisher for their great support to publish the book. I would like to thank them and all who helped and supported me. I dedicate this book to all those who love learning Chinese. I sincerely welcome readers to give me their valuable suggestions and input after reading it.

Li Shujuan

October 5, 2007

前　言

“流行语”是指在某一时期、某一地域出现，并且广为流行的语汇。这些语汇多为创新的或从外语引进的，有些语汇则是旧瓶装新酒，在其原本的语义上引申出新的含义，有些则是借用了方言、俚语、行话。因此，流行语具有强烈的时代感和地域特征。

流行语的使用范围十分广泛，包含了人们生活的各个方面。在语体上，流行语不仅用于书面语，也可用于口语。

流行语作为最具时代特征的语汇，与社会的发展和演变密切相关。在每一个时代，都会涌现出一批反映社会发展的词汇。近年来，随着改革开放的深入，更多的新词语出现并广为流传，如今，最流行的词语莫过于“八荣八耻”、“和谐社会”、“基民”、“股民”等，这些词汇中无不折射出时代和社会的特点，反映社会的发展进程。当然，正是由于流行语的这一特性，使得词语的变化较快，一些词汇由于时代的变迁而淡出、消亡，成为历史的记忆。

这本书作为一本汉英对照的最新流行汉语词典，收录了二十一世纪以来，特别是近年中国最流行的词汇，其中不仅包括媒体上经常出现的词语，也有一些具有一定代表性和普遍性的网络流行词语，及人们日常生活中熟悉的、常见的词语，内容涉及时政、社会、经济、科技、文体、时尚、网络、工作、学习、生活等各个领域。

本书共收词条近800条，每个词条包括词目、注音、释义和例句。全部词目以汉语拼音注音。每个词目的释义都用英文解释。有多个义项的，则分别用数字符号表示。每个义项后面一般附一个例句，用以准确表示该词语的意义和用法。本书以英文字母顺序排列。以英文字母开头的字母词列于正文最后。

随着汉语在海外不断升温，学习汉语的人越来越多。为了满足学习者的需要，我特地为学习汉语的留学生、海外华人、会汉语的外国人、研究中国问题的外国学者、国外大中学生编写了此书，目的主要在于帮助他们学习和理解在阅读和与人交往中遇到的一些流行语的语义和表达形式。由于本书采用了汉英对照的形式，因此，也对国内从事翻译的人员具有一定的参考作用。

在编写翻译本书过程中，我得到了许多朋友的关心和支持。我特别要感谢社会科学院语言研究所研究员、中国辞书学会副会长兼秘书长韩敬体先生的指导，感谢出版社的编辑和领导的大力协助，使本书的出版得以顺利完成。在此谨向他们和所有帮助和支持过我的人表示最衷心的感谢。愿以此书奉献给一切热爱汉语学习的朋友们。同时，我也热忱希望广大读者朋友对本书提出宝贵意见。

李淑娟

2007年10月5日

目 录 Contents

A

挨宰 ái zǎi

◆ be overcharged, be fleeced

例 你挨宰了,这东西根本不值那么多钱。

► You're overcharged. This thing isn't worth that much.

安检 ān jiǎn

◆ security check

例 把东西放这儿,过一下安检。

► Put your things here to go through the security check.

安居工程 ān jū gōng chéng

◆ Economy Housing Project; housing project for low-income urban residents

This is a Chinese government initiative aimed at solving the housing problems of low-income families. It finances the construction of houses and sells them at cost price or with little profit.

例 近年来,西藏自治区大力实施农牧民"安居工程",惠及广大农牧民。目前已有很多农牧民住上了新居。

► In recent years, the Tibetan Autonomous Region has implemented the Economy Housing Project, bringing benefits to farmers and herdsmen. At present many farmers and herdsmen have moved into new houses.

A

安乐死 ān lè sǐ

◆ euthanasia

例 2002年荷兰通过了一项“安乐死法案”,成为世界上第一个安乐死合法化的国家。

▶ In 2002 the Netherlands passed a euthanasia law, and became the first country to legalize euthanasia.

按揭 àn jiē

◆ mortgage

例 越来越多的人通过购买按揭房改变了住房环境，但与此同时也有一大批人,特别是年轻人成为了新一代的“负翁”。

▶ More and more people have changed their living conditions by buying houses on mortgage. However, this has caused a great number of people, especially the young to become debtors of the new generation.

暗访 àn fǎng

◆ interview secretly

例 记者用暗访的方式获取新闻信息,对新闻进行最深度的报道。

▶ Having gained the information by way of a secret interview, the correspondent made a most deep and thorough report on the incidents.

暗箱操作 àn xiāng cāo zuò

◆ black case work; do something stealthily by using one's power in order to seek huge profits

例 为了防止组织者进行暗箱操作，大赛组委会特聘公证员参与每场比赛，对大赛进行监督。

▶ In order to prevent black casework of organizers, the organizing committee of the competition has invited registrars to take part in every game supervising the whole process.

奥运 ào yùn

◆ Olympic Games

例 “绿色奥运、科技奥运、人文奥运”是2008年北京奥运会的理念。

▶ Green Olympics, Scientific Olympics and Humanistic Olympics are the themes of Beijing Olympic Games in 2008.

B

B

80后 bā líng hòu

◆ people born in the 1980s

例 这本书的作者是活跃在文坛上的80后写手，所以非常受年轻读者的欢迎。

▶ The author of this book is a writer active in literary circles and was born in the 1980s. This makes him very popular among young readers.

八卦新闻 bā guà xīn wén

◆ gossip or fluffy news

例 这种小报专门登一些八卦新闻吸引读者。

▶ These tabloids only publish gossip or fluffy news to attract readers.

八卦 bā guà

◆ 1. rumor, gossip

例 很多人都爱听八卦，不管真假，大家就图一乐吧，并没有多少人去较真儿。

▶ Many people love to listen to rumors. It matters not if the rumors are true. It's just for fun. Nobody treats it seriously.

◆ 2. be good at gossip

例 他这个人太八卦了，所以别把他的话当真。

▶ He is good at gossip, so don't take his words seriously.

八荣八耻 bā róng bā chǐ

◆ socialist concept of honor and disgrace—Eight Dos and Don'ts

例 胡锦涛主席提出的以"八荣八耻"为主要内容的社会主义荣辱观，是对马克思主义道德观的精辟概括。

► The socialist concept of honor and disgrace, "Eight Dos and Don'ts" proposed by President Hu Jintao is an incisive summary to the moral concept of Marxism.

吧女 bā nǚ

◆ bar girl

例 为了能多挣些钱，阿美白天在工厂里打工，晚上去做吧女。

► A'mei works in a factory during the day, and works as a bar girl in the evening to make more money.

吧台 bā tái

◆ bar counter

例 在吧台旁坐着喝酒的那名男子就是昨天在电视上看到的那个歌手。

► That man sitting at the bar drinking is the singer we saw on TV yesterday.

把脉 bǎ mài

◆ feel the pulse; a metaphor for conducting a survey, analysis and evaluation

例 这家工厂的产品总是销路不好，因此，厂领导请来两位专家来把脉，希望尽快能找出解决的办法。

B

► The products of this factory don't sell very well, so the leaders of the factory invited two experts to give their analysis and evaluation in hope of finding a solution as soon as possible.

霸王条款 bà wáng tiáo kuǎn

◆ arbitrary clause, no-traded clause (NTC)

例 中国消费者协会公布了首批霸王条款后，在社会上引起了巨大反响。

► After the China Consumer Association publicized the first group of arbitrary clauses, it provoked a great response by society.

掰 bāi

◆ break up; break off a friendship

例 汤姆和史蒂夫在发生了一次激烈的争吵后,两个人就掰了。

► Tom broke his friendship with Steve after an argument.

白搭 bái dā

◆ It's no use; futile; exert effort in vain

例 这种事你就是找到他也白搭,他肯定不会承认他与这件事有关。

► It's no use blaming him for such a thing because he definitely won't admit he has anything to do with it.

白骨精 bái gǔ jīng

◆ an abbreviation for white collar, cadre, and elite

This is the name of a siren in the famous Chinese novel *Journey to the West*. But today it is also used as a new term for white-collar office workers who excel in their career.

B

例 既然你有志要当一名未来的“白骨精”，现在为何不努力学习呢？

▶ Since you are determined to be a successful white-collar worker in the future, why don't you study hard now?

白话 bái hua

◆ make empty talk; talk big; talk nonsense; blah-blah

例 这个人特别能白话。不过，他的话你可不能全信。

▶ This person is very talkative, but you can't fully believe his words.

白金唱片 bái jīn chàng piàn

◆ 1. record sales over one million copies

例 今年 8 月他的首张专辑在韩国和新西兰获得白金唱片。

▶ In August this year, his first album sold one million copies in South Korea and New Zealand.

◆ 2. platinum Album Award

例 拥有 21 次金唱片奖和 4 次白金唱片奖的约翰·丹佛是中国观众最熟悉的美国乡村歌手之一。

▶ John Denver, who received 21 Gold Album Awards and 4 Platinum Album Awards, is one of the best known US country music singers in China.

白领 bái lǐng

◆ white collar

例 他想做白领，在高级写字楼里上班，不想像他的父母那样靠干农活为生。

▶ He wants to become a white-collar worker and works in a modern office building. He doesn't want to be a farmer like his parents.

B

白领犯罪 bái lǐng fàn zuì

◆ white-collar crime

例 随着科技的发展，白领犯罪呈上升趋势。

► Along with the development of science and technology, white-collar crime is following an upward trend.

白色垃圾 bái sè lā jī

◆ white garbage

例 这两年，经过环境治理，这一带的白色垃圾已经越来越少。

► Over the past two years, with environmental improvements, white garbage in this area has decreased.

白色收入 bái sè shōu rù

◆ legal income

例 他的白色收入本来就不少，再加上各种灰色收入，养车养房他是绝对没有问题。

► His legal income alone is not bad. With the addition of his other income, he has no problem at all maintaining a car and a house.

白色污染 bái sè wū rǎn

◆ white pollution

例 这里的白色污染日趋严重，已经引起了有关方面的高度重视，他们正采取有力措施改变这一局面。

► White pollution is getting worse and worse here, catching the serious scrutiny of relevant departments. They are taking strong measures to correct this situation.

百家讲坛 bǎi jiā jiǎng tán

◆ a forum program broadcast on CCTV, a platform to spread the knowledge of interesting people

例《百家讲坛》是中央电视台推出的一个大型教育系列节目，许多教授通过上这个节目而一炮走红。

► The *Baijia Forum* program is an educational series broadcast by CCTV. Many professors have become famous soon after giving lectures on this program.

摆平 bǎi píng

◆ 1. solve the problem, strike a balance; be even-handed

例 这事只有他出面才能摆平，他在这行儿享有很高的威信。

► This matter can't be treated fairly unless he comes. He enjoys a high reputation in this field.

◆ 2. punish

例 他也太狂了，看来你得亲自出马摆平他了。

► He is too arrogant. It seems you must punish him yourself.

摆谱 bǎi pǔ

◆ keep up appearances, go in for extravagance, show off one's wealth

例 好莱坞的明星真能摆谱，一个婚礼就能花一百多万美元。

► Hollywood stars are good at showing off their wealth. They can spend a million dollars on a wedding.

摆摊儿 bǎi tānr

◆ set up a vendor stall along the street or in a market

例 退休后他去摆摊儿卖金鱼了。

► He set up a stall to sell goldfish after he retired.

斑竹 bān zhú

◆ board moderator

A moderator is a person who watches an Internet message board system and deletes posts that break the rules, move threads, etc. The Chinese word for mottled bamboo has the same pronunciation as the word for moderator.

例 这个网上论坛的斑竹受到网友的欢迎。

► The moderator of the forum is quite populor among the net friends.

板儿寸 bǎnr cùn

◆ hairstyle of which the hair is cropped close to the head; closely cropped hair; bush-top

例 夏天男人们都喜欢留板儿寸，凉快，而且看上去格外精神。

► In summer men like to wear the bush-top. It is nice and cool, and looks very smart.

板凳 bǎn dèng

◆ wooden stool

This is a term referring to the third person in a network responding to a message. The pronunciation is the same as for the Chinese word for bench.

例 真遗憾！今天我上线晚了，只抢到了个板凳。

► What a pity! I got online late and only got a stool today.

板凳队员 bǎn dèng duì yuán

◆ be an alternate player of a team

例 他在球队三个月了，可是一直是板凳队员。这让他不免有些郁闷。

▶ He's been on the team for three months, but he is still an alternate player, which makes him feel a bit gloomy.

版主 bǎn zhǔ

◆ mod (moderator) of BBS forum

例 最近，艾瑞克在网络上出了个小风头，在《读书生活》论坛上当了半年轮值版主。

▶ Eric has recently found online fame serving as a Mod on *Reading Life Forum* for six months.

扮靓 bàn liàng

◆ 1. make beautiful; beautify

例 为了吸引异性的目光，扮靓自己是她每天必做的事。

▶ In order to catch men's attention, she must beautify herself every day.

◆ 2. make something look pretty and neat through decoration or cleaning up

例 国庆节期间，上百万盆鲜花组成的花坛扮靓了这个城市的大街小巷。

▶ During National Day, arrangements including millions of pots of flowers make the streets of the city more beautiful.

扮酷 bàn kù

◆ play it cool

例 今天的年轻男士们都喜欢扮酷。

► The young men today like to play it cool.

傍 bàng

◆ 1. rely on or accompany a person who is rich, useful or has a certain social position

例 她专傍老外寻机出国。

► She goes around with foreigners in the hopes of getting a chance to go abroad.

◆ 2. love, have an intimate relationship with someone

例 他们俩傍了一年了,不知道的人还以为他们是夫妻呢。

► They have had a relationship for over a year. One who doesn't know them might think they are a couple.

棒槌 bàng chui

◆ wooden club (used in the old days to beat clothes when washing them); a metaphor for a layman or an amateur

例 在出版这行儿里我可是个棒槌。

► I'm an amateur in the publishing field.

棒杀 bàng shā

◆ hit or strike severely without knowing right from wrong, scorn without full knowledge of something

例 张艺谋的新片刚出来就立刻遭到媒体的棒杀。

► Zhang Yimou's new film just came out and was immediately scorned by the media.

包装 bāo zhuāng

◆ package; a metaphor for beautifying or enhancing a person or a thing

例 现在什么都得讲究包装。如果你想找到一个好工作,就得从简历到个人整体形象都好好把自己包装一下。

▶ Nowadays everything focuses on packaging. If you want to find a good job, you have to package yourself from your resume to your personal presentation.

煲电话粥 bāo diàn huà zhōu

◆ cook porridge on the telephone; a metaphor for talking on the phone too long

例 她总爱煲电话粥,所以她每月要支付很高的电话费。

▶ She always cooks porridge on the phone so she spends a lot of money paying her telephone bill.

保廉 bǎo lián

◆ keep probity

例 新一届领导班子提出建立反腐保廉预防体系的构想。

▶ The new leading group proposed setting up a preventive system for anti-corruption and keeping probity.

保送 bǎo sòng

◆ recommend for the admission to a higher-level school

例 不少获得奥运冠军的中国运动员被保送进入国内一流大学学习。

▶ Many Chinese athletes who won the Olympic championships have been recommended for admission to the best colleges or universities in the country.

暴走 bào zǒu

◆ walk swiftly

例 这个小花园每天晚上都有一些人在这里暴走，锻炼身体。

► Every evening in this small garden there are people walking swiftly for exercise.

暴堵 bào dǔ

◆ traffic jam

This is also a homophone of a Beijing special snack named 爆肚.

例 今天是周一，一大早京城街头就出现交通暴堵现象。

► Today is Monday. Early in the morning there was a traffic jam in Beijing.

爆炒 bào chǎo

◆ quick-fry; a metaphor for launching a whirlwind mass media advertising campaign for quick and optimum commercial impact in a short period

例 新片还未上映，电影公司对此片的爆炒就已经开始了，以吸引更多媒体的注意。

► Before the new film hit the theaters, the film company had already started to quick-fry it in order to arouse more media attention.

爆棚 bào péng

◆ literally meaning a tent that is too crowded with people and may explode; a metaphor for something that is so popular and loved by people so that many wish to join it or go to it

例 历时两天的秋季招聘会刚刚开始，就出现了爆棚，许多姗姗来迟的人不得不在外面排队等候。

► The two-day autumn job-hunting fair has just started and it's already crowded. Many people who came late had to queue outside.

背包族 bēi bāo zú

◆ backpacker

例 作为一名"背包族",除了热情和勇气之外,在出发前你还应了解一些与旅游有关的知识。

► As a backpacker, besides having enthusiasm and courage, you should also have some relevant knowledge before setting out.

北漂 běi piāo

◆ 1. to come to Beijing and lead an unsettled life there

例 北漂的日子最初非常苦,但大多数人都艰难地挺过来了,最终实现了自己的梦想。

► The first days after arriving in Beijing and being unsettled were very hard. But most people who persevered finally had their dreams come true.

◆ 2. artists, actors and artisans who come to cities in northern China, particularly Beijing, to develop their careers

例 不少明星都是北漂,其中最有代表性的就是张国立和邓捷。

► Many stars have come to Beijing for personal development. Among them, Zhang Guoli and Deng Jie are the most famous.

备不住 bèi bú zhù

◆ perhaps, maybe

例 你怎么这时候才来,备不住他等不到你已经先走了。

► Why have you came at this time (so late), perhaps he couldn't wait so long and had already left without you.

背 bèi

◆ be unlucky; have bad luck

例 我最近特背，每次玩牌都输。

► I'm very unlucky lately. Every time I play cards, I lose.

B

背投 bèi tóu

◆ rear projection screen

例 近年来，背投、等离子(PDP)、液晶电视(LCD TV)的跃然而出，让高端彩电的王位几易其主。

► In recent years, the launch of new products such as rear projection TV, plasma display projection (PDP) and liquid crystal display (LCD) TV have taken the throne of high-level color television production.

倍儿棒 bèir bàng

◆ exceptionally good, great

例 这个小伙子倍儿棒，要个儿有个儿，要长相有长相。

► This lad is great. He's both tall and handsome.

蹦迪 bèng dí

◆ disco dance

例 周末，去蹦迪的人还真不少，年轻人居多。

► On weekends, many people go to dance at the discos. Most are young men.

蹦极 bèng jí

◆ bungee jumping

例 蹦极是一项年轻人的运动，需要足够的勇气和胆量。

► Bungee jumping is a sport for the young. It needs courage and guts.

比拼 bǐ pīn

◆ both sides strive to compete with all energy

例 在厨艺挑战赛上，两名选手在台上比拼才艺。

► Two players contest their talent and cooking skill on the stage.

边缘化 biān yuán huà

◆ be at the fringe of society, be ignored by mainstream society

例 一些政策导致了一个人们不愿看到的结果：职业教育被边缘化了。

► A series of policies has caused a result people don't want to see: vocational education is ignored by mainstream society.

扁 biǎn

◆ beat, hit, strike

例 他又骂人了，也许是不甘寂寞想让人来扁他一顿，他才老实。

► He has come out again to scold people. Perhaps he is unwilling to live an obscure life and is looking for some trouble by getting others to attack him.

飙升 biāo shēng

◆ soar, rocket

例 近来股市一路飙升，吸引了众多的新股民入市。

► Recently, the soaring stock market has attracted a lot of new investors to the market.

并购 bìng gòu

◆ merger and acquisition

例 近年来,并购已成为中国经济中的一个热门话题。

► Mergers and acquisitions have become a hot topic in the Chinese economy in recent years.

并轨 bìng guǐ

◆ combination of two methods

例 1994 年,中国开始施行人民币汇率并轨。

► In 1994, China began to implement the unification of Chinese currency exchange rates.

病毒 bìng dú

◆ virus

例 近日网络上流行一种新病毒,致使许多电脑中毒瘫痪。

► Recently, a new virus has emerged on the Internet, causing many computers to crash.

博彩 bó cǎi

◆ gamble

例 这个网站每天都提供博彩资讯。

► This website provides gambling information every day.

博客 bó kè

◆ blog

例 许多人都有自己的博客,并把写博客当做生活中的一件趣事来做。

► Many people have their own blogs and consider them to be an interesting thing in their life.

不待见 bú dài jian

◆ annoy, dislike

例 你站在这里干什么？还不赶紧走，省得招人不待见。

▶ What are you doing by standing here? Go quickly in case others dislike you.

不靠谱 bú kào pǔ

◆ not accurate or reliable in speech or action

例 这么重要的事怎么能让他去办呢？ 他这人办事可不靠谱。

▶ How could you let him do such an important thing? He is not reliable.

不吝 bú lìn

◆ not care, not mind

例 他这人胆子就是大，什么事情都不吝。

▶ He is very bold and doesn't care.

不着调儿 bù zháo diàor

◆ have no relation (to a solution); have nothing to do with

例 别竟说些不着调儿的话，来点实际的行动。

▶ Don't just talk about it. Do something about it.

步行街 bù xíng jiē

◆ walking street

例 这条街是步行街，所有车辆都得绕行。

▶ This is a walking street for pedestrians. All vehicles must make a detour.

C

C

擦边球 cā biān qiú

◆ line ball; a metaphor for something close to the edge of a policy, but not quite against the policy

例 有些人特别会钻空子，总爱打法律的擦边球。

► Some people are extremely good at exploiting an advantage and always play line ball with the law.

彩铃 cǎi líng

◆ ring tone (for cell phones)

例 这个网站能提供最专业、最热门的手机彩铃。

► This website can provide the most professional and the most popular mobile phone ring tones.

彩民 cǎi mín

◆ lottery ticket buyer

例 体育彩票给市民的生活带来了新的乐趣，许多彩民天天都买彩票，希望有一天能中大奖。

► Sports lotteries have brought new pleasure to people's lives. Many buy tickets everyday in the hope of hitting the jackpot.

彩票 cǎi piào

◆ lottery

例 他只是偶尔买张彩票，试试运气。

► He only buys a lottery ticket once in a while to try his luck.

菜篮子 cài lán zi

◆ vegetable basket

It refers to the vegetables and subsidiary food supplied to urban citizens.

例 为了保证市民的"菜篮子"安全,市政府在郊区建设了一个绿色农产品基地。

► In order to ensure the safety of "vegetable baskets" of the citizens, the city government has built up a green agricultural product base in the suburbs.

菜鸟 cài niǎo

◆ new hand, greenhorn, rookie

例 他刚学了几天电脑,还是个菜鸟,所以,你对他一定要有耐心才行。

► He has just started learning the computer these last few days and is still a rookie, so you must be patient with him.

参与度 cān yù dù

◆ degree of participation in all activities, expressing one's opinions on the problems or matters

例 随着环保意识的增强,人们对环保问题的参与度正在明显增强。

► With growing awareness of the need for environmental protection, the degree of people's participation in working to solve environmental problems is increasing.

惨 cǎn

◆ 1. awkward, pitiful, miserable

C

C

例 今天我可真惨，上班第一天就把手机给丢了。

► I had a miserable day today. I lost my mobile phone on the first day of work.

◆ 2. (looking) bad, poor

例 说实话，这小伙子人真不错，就是长得惨点。

Frankly speaking, this lad is pretty good, except for his bad looks.

草根 cǎo gēn

◆ grass roots

例 他对媒体从不回避自己的草根出身，并以此为荣。

► He never hides his grass roots background from the media, and is actually proud of it.

草根文化 cǎo gēn wén huà

◆ grass-root culture, populace's culture

例 相声算不上是高雅艺术，只能说是一种草根文化。

► Crosstalk is not considered as an elegant art, but a kind of grass-root culture.

蹭吃喝 cèng chī hē

◆ get something free to eat and drink

例 这人特没劲，除了跟朋友蹭吃喝，什么忙都帮不上。

► He is really good-for-nothing except getting a free meal or drink from you.

蹭饭 cèng fàn

◆ get a free meal

例 你这么晚来这儿,是想蹭饭的吧?

▶ Do you intend to get a free meal from me by coming to see me at this time of the day?

插足 chā zú

◆ 1. gain a foothold, put one's foot in

例 她的家里到处都是书,床上、地上,几乎没有地方插足了。

▶ Her home is full of books, on the bed and the floor, such that there's almost no room to put your feet.

◆ 2. get involved

例 有不少人离婚是因为第三者插足造成的。

▶ Many people get divorced because of the involvement of a third party.

茶吧 chá bā

◆ tea bar, teahouse

例 这条街上有不少茶吧,有中国人开的,也有外国人开的。

▶ There are many teahouses on this street. Some are run by Chinese, and some by foreigners.

茶艺 chá yì

◆ skill of making tea, art of tea

例 这里的服务员都学过茶艺,看她们为你沏茶也是一种享受。

▶ All the waitresses here have learnt the art of tea. It's a joy to watch them making tea for you.

拆迁 chāi qiān

◆ raze old houses and resettle the inhabitants

例 由于道路扩建,城里有不少旧房屋需要拆迁。

► Because of projects involving widening of roads, many old houses will be razed and the occupants resettled.

C

超女 chāo nǚ

◆ super girl

Originally, *Super Girl* was the title of a TV program now called *Star Selection*. Now it is an abbreviation for the girls performing on the program.

例 她是从超女比赛中脱颖而出的,如今已经出了三张音乐专辑。

► She gained fame on a *Super Girl Contest*. Now she has recorded three music albums.

超前 chāo qián

◆ transcending the present; ahead of the times

例 他们生产的这个产品有些超前,不能被大多数人接受,这影响了产品销量。

► Their product is somewhat ahead of the times and most people can't get it. This factor affects the sales of the product.

超前消费 chāo qián xiāo fèi

◆ unduly high level of consumption; over consumption; excessive consumption, premature consumption

例 多数年轻人都喜欢超前消费,他们的消费水平也很高,特别是在汽车和奢侈品方面。

► Most young people enjoy over consumption. Their consumption level is very high, especially in cars and luxury goods.

C

炒股 chǎo gǔ

◆ engage in stock market investment, buy and resell stocks at a profit

例 他把所有的钱都拿去炒股了。

▶ He invested all his money in stocks.

炒汇 chǎo huì

◆ arbitrage; buy and resell foreign currency at a profit

例 他整日忙着炒汇,挣了不少钱。

▶ He is busy all day buying and reselling foreign currency, earning a lot of money.

炒家 chǎo jiā

◆ skillful broker or speculator

例 新股上市吸引来了很多炒家。

▶ New stocks coming into the market have attracted many skillful speculators.

炒楼花 chǎo lóu huā

◆ investment in a building which is under construction

例 股票下跌后,不少人就去炒楼花了。

▶ After stocks went down, many people shifted their investment to construction.

炒邮 chǎo yóu

◆ investment in stamps; buy and resell stamps

C

例 他专门从事炒邮，这些年赚了不少钱。

▶ He invests in stamps and has earned a lot of money in recent years.

炒鱿鱼 chǎo yóu yú

◆ sack, dismiss, fire

例 他因为得罪了一个大客户，被老板炒鱿鱼了。

▶ His boss fired him because he offended a big client.

炒作 chǎo zuò

◆ promote, publicize; make something known to the public

例 人们认为她想通过打这场官司来炒作她的新影片。

▶ People think that she aims to promote her new movie by engaging in a lawsuit.

扯皮 chě pí

◆ dispute over trifles; argue back and forth; wrangle

例 这点小事就别扯皮了，你来定吧。

▶ Don't argue back and forth for such trifles. You must decide.

诚信 chéng xìn

◆ faith, honesty

例 无论做人还是经商都应该讲诚信，这样才能形成良好的社会风气。

▶ One should pay attention to his credibility, either personally or in business, as this can help to form a healthy social atmosphere.

吃不了兜着走 chī bù liǎo dōu zhe zǒu

◆ 1. ask for a "doggy bag"; take one's leftovers back home

例 你多点几个菜。不用担心,吃不了我兜着走。

► Order more dishes, please. Don't worry, I'll ask for a doggy bag if there is any food left.

◆ 2. get more than one bargained for; land oneself in serious trouble

例 这件事关系重大,一旦出问题,你可是要吃不了兜着走。

► This matter is very serious. If there is any problem, you will have a big trouble.

吃醋 chī cù

◆ be jealous

例 在她面前可不能夸别的女人漂亮,不然,她会吃醋的。

► You can't praise other women for their beauty in front of her, otherwise she'll be jealous.

吃错药 chī cuò yào

◆ take the wrong medicine; a term infers a person's behavior is a bit strange or rude and impolite

例 我怀疑她今天是吃错药了,否则不会对我发这么大的火。

► I wonder if she has taken the wrong medicine today, otherwise she wouldn't have been so angry with me.

吃回扣 chī huí kòu

◆ accept a commission

例 1. 一些行业有吃回扣现象,这已经成为一种社会的弊端。

► Accepting a commission is common in some walks of life. It has become a social malpractice.

C

例 2. 他总让人把书交给这家工厂来印,一定没少吃回扣。

► He always asks people to have their books printed in that factory. He must receive a lot of commission from them.

吃请 chī qǐng

◆ accept an invitation to dinner

例 除了工作之外,他拒绝任何吃请。

► He refuses any invitation to dinner except for working.

吃香 chī xiāng

◆ be in great demand, be popular, be much sought-after

例 前些年学会计的人特别吃香,他们很容易找到工作。

► A few years ago, accountants were in great demand. It was very easy for them to find a job.

吃心 chī xīn

◆ be suspicious, be oversensitive

例 她这个人很难交往,你跟她说什么,她都特别容易吃心。

► She is very hard to deal with. No matter what you say to her, she is very easy to become suspicious.

持币观望 chí bì guān wàng

◆ hold on to your money and wait and see; wait to invest

例 听说汽车年底要降价，许多想买车的人都在持币观望。

► Hearing that the price of cars will drop at the end of the year, many buyers are holding on to their money until then.

持卡族 chí kǎ zú

◆ (credit) cardholders

例 许多大学生成了持卡族，他们持卡消费的水平很高。

► Many college students have become cardholders. With the cards, their consumption level has become very high.

斥资 chì zī

◆ pay the expenses

例 这家工厂今年斥资上千万元从国外引进了一批最先进的机器。

► This year the factory paid more than ten million yuan to buy the most advanced machines from abroad.

赤潮 chì cháo

◆ red tide

例 仅 2003 年一年，中国海域就发生了 119 次赤潮。

► In 2003 alone, red tides were recorded 119 times in China's seas.

重塑 chóng sù

◆ recreate, reshape, remold

例 Oracle 公司开始踏上了重塑自我的道路。

► Oracle Company started to step on the road of reshaping itself.

重组 chóng zǔ

◆ reorganize, reform

例 1. 资产重组

▶ reorganize assets

例 2. 电信业重组涉及至少三个大问题。

▶ The reform of telecom industry is confronted with at least three big problems.

例 3. 民营企业应走强强合并与重组的道路。

▶ Privately owned enterprises should pursue reorganizing and merging with strong companies.

臭脚 chòu jiǎo

◆ 1. (of football) bad play

例 臭脚,这么好的机会他还没踢进球。

▶ Bad play, he lost such a good chance.

◆ 2. (of football) poor player

例 他的球踢得可差了,是班上有名的臭脚。

▶ He plays soccer very badly. He is well known as a poor player in his class.

臭街了 chòu jiē le

◆ literally "stink the street"; a fad or craze

例 手机现在都臭街了,连收废品的人都用手机来联系业务。

▶ Mobile phones are a very popular craze, even scrap collectors use mobile phones to get business.

出彩儿 chū cǎir

◆ make something excellent; do brilliant things

C

例 1. 为了让这部电影更出彩儿，导演找来了近来最红的影星出演主角。

▶ In order to make the movie more excellent, the director found a most popular movie star to play the leading role.

例 2. 电视剧倒是不少，可特别出彩儿的并不太多。

▶ There are many TV shows, but extremely excellent ones are very few.

例 3. 年轻的演员们演得非常出彩儿。

▶ The young actors played very well.

出手 chū shǒu

◆ 1. give someone a hand; help

例 在他最困难的时候，多亏公司出手，他才渡过了难关。

▶ He was deep in trouble. Thanks to the company who helped him, he finally overcame his difficulties.

◆ 2. produce, offer, invest

例 这个项目由于有着巨大的市场回报潜能，因此吸引了大量港澳投资商出手。

▶ Since this project has huge potential market returns, it has attracted many investors from Hong Kong and Macao.

◆ 3. sell, get off one's hands

例 他的房子一直没有出手，因为他在等更好的买主。

▶ He hasn't sold his house because he's still waiting for a better buyer.

触电 chù diàn

◆ have one's first experience on TV or in a movie; to play a role in a TV drama or a film, or to be a host / hostess on TV

例 她第一次触电是在她上小学的时候，那时她并没想到从此会与影视表演结缘。

► She played her first role in a TV drama when she was in primary school. At that time she didn't know she would become a regular film and television performer.

春晚 chūn wǎn

◆ televised evening variety show for the Spring Festival; CCTV Spring Festival Gala

例 人们对春晚的热情已不像从前那么高，毕竟如今可选择的娱乐活动和节目多了。

► People's enthusiasm for the evening show of the Spring Festival is no longer as high as before. Today, the selective entertainment activities and programs are getting more repetitive.

纯天然 chún tiān rán

◆ pure natural

例 纯天然的东西越来越受消费者的欢迎。

► people love pure and natural things more and more.

磁悬浮列车 cí xuán fú liè chē

◆ maglev train (magnetically levitated train); magnetic suspension train

例 中国自主研制的第一辆磁悬浮列车首次在上海亮相。

► The first domestically developed and produced maglev train in China made its debut in Shanghai.

刺儿头 cìr tóu

◆ troublesome or difficult person

例 他是单位有名的刺儿头，没有人愿意与他打交道。

▶ He is well known as a troublesome person in his unit. Nobody likes to deal with him.

凑份子 còu fèn zi

◆ 1. band together to buy a present for someone

例 如今办喜事不兴凑份子，大家都给新人红包了。

▶ Nowadays shopping together to buy a present for the newly-weds is not the fashion. Everyone gives a red envelope to the newly-weds instead.

◆ 2. add to the trouble, especially by poking one's nose into others' business

例 人家一搞什么活动，他准来凑份子，跟着瞎掺和。

▶ When someone hosts an activity, he always comes along to make trouble, poking his nose into it.

促销 cù xiāo

◆ promote the sales of goods; sales promotion

例 逢年过节，商店都搞促销活动，还将营业时间延长到夜里 12 点。

▶ On holiday occasions, all shops have sales promotions, and extend their working time to 12 o'clock at night.

攒电脑 cuán diàn nǎo

◆ assemble a computer

例 他攒电脑已经好多年了，他攒的电脑质量好，而且还便宜。

▶ He has assembled computers for many years. All the computers he has assembled are inexpensive and of good quality.

窜红 cuàn hóng

◆ become famous or popular quickly

例 她是这两年窜红的歌星。

► She is a singing star who has become popular in just two years.

寸头 cùn tóu

◆ crew cut

例 他在新片中一改往日的造型，将长发改为寸头，令人眼前一亮。

► He changed his former hairstyle for the new movie looking cool with a crew cut, making everyone look at him with new eyes.

搓火 cuō huǒ

◆ get angry; feel impatient; irritate

例 他干的这事真让人搓火。

► The thing he did is really irritating.

撮 cuō

◆ eat; have a meal

例 咱们好不容易才见个面，还不好好地撮一顿，叙叙旧？

► It's not been easy for us to see each other lately. Why not go out for a big meal and have a good chat?

D

D

打白条 dǎ bái tiáo

◆ write an IOU, write a note signed in acknowledgement of a debt

例 又到收购粮食的时候了，今年中央三令五申不许再出现给农民打白条的现象。

▶ It's time for purchasing grain again. This year, the central government has repeatedly ordered buyers not to write IOUs to farmers.

打车（的）dǎ chē (dí)

◆ take a taxi

例 时间来不及了，你还是赶紧打车去吧。

▶ There is no time. You'd better run and take a taxi.

打工妹 dǎ gōng mèi

◆ young woman, usually from the countryside, working in the city

例 这是一部反映打工妹在深圳工作和生活的影片。

▶ This is a film reflecting the life of young working women in Shenzhen.

打工仔 dǎ gōng zǎi

◆ young man, usually from the countryside, working in the city

例 他原来只是一名打工仔，如今已成了一家公司的老板。

▶ He used to be a young employee. Today, he has become the boss of a company.

打黑 dǎ hēi

◆ the cracking down on the criminal activities of underworld gangs

例 市政府把“打黑”作为近期的主要工作。

▶ The municipal government considers the work of cracking down on the criminal activities of underworld gangs as its recent major task.

打假 dǎ jiǎ

◆ stamp out counterfeit goods

例 各部门的“打假”工作从来就没有停止过。

▶ The work of stamping out counterfeit goods has never stopped.

大跌眼镜 dà diē yǎn jìng

◆ have one's glasses falling off; a metaphor for something very surprising or unexpected

例 这款产品的销量如此之高,令不少业内人士大跌眼镜。

▶ The sales of this product are so high that it has greatly surprised many people of the trade.

大鳄 dà è

◆ huge crocodile; a metaphor for the most powerful person or organ in real estate, finance or other fields or industries

例 金融大鳄以其气魄和实力影响股票市场的涨跌走势。

▶ The huge finance crocodiles influence the rise and fall of stock markets with their boldness and strength.

大放送 dà fàng sòng

◆ 1. on sale, sales promotion

例 那家店正在搞冰箱大放送。

► That shop is having a sales promotion on refrigerators.

大换血 dà huàn xiě

◆ change blood; a metaphor to adjust and change members on a large scale

例 中国女排经过这次大换血后,队员的平均年龄降低了五六岁。

► After the Chinese Women's Volleyball Team changed blood this time, the average age of players went down five or six years.

大款 dà kuǎn

◆ very rich person, big wheel, money bag

例 公司老总个个都是大款,从他们开的车你就能看出来。

► Bosses of companies are all money bags. You can see this by the cars they drive.

大卖场 dà mài chǎng

◆ hypermarket, super center, warehouse market

例 这本书在成都的几个大卖场里都销售得不错。

► This book sells pretty well in several hypermarkets in Chengdu.

大派送 dà pài sòng

◆ give something free in large quantities

例 在情人节这天,商场门前的玫瑰大派送引来不少顾客。

▶ On Valentine's Day, giving free roses in front of the department stores attracted many customers.

大片儿 dà piānr

D

◆ big budget films that saw great box-office success

例 年底将有两部美国大片儿和四部国产影片在全国影院放映。

▶ At the end of the year, two American big budget successful films and four Chinese movies will be shown in cinemas across the country.

大手笔 dà shǒu bǐ

◆ large-scale, very creative and influential measure or action

例 邓小平提出的"改革开放"可以说是中国历史上的一个大手笔。

▶ Deng Xiaoping's economic reform and opening to the outside world can be considered as a large-scale, very creative and influential measure in Chinese history.

大腕儿 dà wànr

◆ famous person, big shot, expert, celebrity (mostly used in entertainment field)

例 这次音乐盛典的颁奖晚会由于少了许多大腕儿的出席而变得黯然失色。

▶ The grand ceremony of the musical award evening party was dimed by the absence of many celebrities.

单身贵族 dān shēn guì zú

◆ single aristocrat; a metaphor for single well-off person

例 这两年,城市中单身贵族的数量日益增多,这已成为一种流行趋势。

▶ In the past two years, the number of single aristocrats in cities has increased, and it has become vogue.

淡出 dàn chū

◆ leave (a career) without notice; gradually disappear; fade out

例 他早已淡出歌坛，专心经营他的生意去了。

▶ He abandoned singing long ago, and has engaged himself in doing business.

蛋白质 dàn bái zhì

◆ abbreviation for a foolish, idiotic or neurotic person or thing (derogatory)

例 那个地方的女人都多多少少有些蛋白质，她们不大用脑子，尤其遇到感情问题，更是好比一团浆糊，一辈子都不可能活明白。

▶ The women in that place are foolish, idiotic and neurotic. They don't use their brains or think clearly especially when they encounter emotional problems. They may never understand it themselves for their whole life.

当红 dāng hóng

◆ be in favor, be in vogue; popular

例 开幕式上当红歌星纷纷亮相并登台献艺。

▶ At the opening ceremony, popular singers get on stage and perform.

导购 dǎo gòu

◆ salesperson who provides guidance (for purchase)

例 在大商场里，导购随时为你提供购物方面的帮助。

D

▶ In large department stores there are some salespersons girls to help you with guidance for your purchase at any time.

倒胃口 dǎo wèi kǒu

D

◆ 1. spoil one's appetite, upset one's stomach

例 吃饭的时候你说这么恶心的话题，真让人倒胃口。

▶ The disgusting topics you talked about while eating really spoiled my appetite.

◆ 2. kill one's interest, dampen one's spirits; be boring

例 这本书的封面让人看了就倒胃口，谁还想买呀？

▶ The cover of this book is so boring at first glance. Who would want to buy it?

灯泡儿 dēng pàor

◆ bulb; a metaphor for third wheel

例 你们俩去谈你们的吧，我可不想在旁边做灯泡儿。

▶ You go yourselves. I don't want to be a third wheel.

低保 dī bǎo

◆ low (minimal) assurance; government provided assistance for low income families

例 中国最近提高了社会低保发放标准。

▶ Recently China raised the standard of granting minimal social assurance.

低调 dī diào

◆ low-key, low profile

例 他一直保持比较低调的生活，不喜欢接受任何媒体的采访。

▶ He always keeps a low-profile life and doesn't like to be interviewed by the media.

地球村 dì qiú cūn

◆ global community, globe (seen as a village)

例 在麦克卢汉看来，"地球村"的主要含义不是指发达的传媒使地球变小了，而是指人们的交往方式以及人的社会和文化形态的重大变化。

▶ In the view of McLuhan, the meaning of "global community" does not refer to the earth getting smaller as the result of a well-developed media, but rather, the great changes in methods of communication, and the conformation of human society and cultures.

地毯式 dì tǎn shì

◆ "carpet searching"; a term meaning a thorough and complete investigation

例 他们对那个村进行地毯式搜索，连只猫都不会跑掉。

▶ They went carpet searching in that village so that even a cat couldn't escape.

第二春 dì èr chūn

◆ second (new) life

例 1. 改革开放给这个地区的发展带来了第二春。

▶ The economic reform and opening to the outside world brought new life to the development of this region.

例 2. 他发誓从零开始，努力创业，实现人生第二春。

▶ He swore he would start from zero and work diligently so as to achieve a new life.

D

颠儿 diānr

◆ go away; leave quickly

例 他一看情况不妙,立刻就颠儿了。

▶ As soon as he saw the situation was not in his favor, he left immediately.

点儿背 diǎnr bèi

◆ bad luck

例 他说他点儿背,刚买了一只股票,第二天就跌了。

▶ He said he had bad luck. He just bought a stock, and the next day it fell.

点击率 diǎn jī lǜ

◆ click-through rate; counter for visitors to an internet web site

例 她的博客点击率已经突破 100 万了。

▶ The click-through rate of her blog is over one million.

电子商务 diàn zǐ shāng wù

◆ e-commerce; electronic commerce

例 这家网站提供电子商务服务。

▶ This website provides e-business service.

电子书 diàn zǐ shū

◆ electronic book

例 人们可以利用 MP4 来看电子书，但它还不会取代人们的传统阅读习惯。

► People can use MP4 to read e-books, but it still can't replace the traditional reading habits of people.

电子眼 diàn zǐ yǎn

◆ electronic eye

例 1. 在现代生活中,电子眼正发挥着越来越大的作用。

► The electronic eye is playing an increasingly important role in modern life.

例 2. 他开车闯红灯被电子眼拍到了。

► He was caught by an electronic eye when he drove against a red light.

吊胃口 diào wèi kǒu

◆ whet one's appetite; hold in suspense; tantalize

例 出什么事了? 你快说吧,就别吊我们大家的胃口了。

► What's up? Please tell us quickly, and don't keep us in suspense.

掉价 diào jià

◆ 1. (of price) go down; fall or drop in price

例 笔记本电脑最近掉价了,比过去便宜了好几百元。

► The price of laptops has dropped recently. It's several hundred yuan lower than before.

◆ 2. lower one's social status, lose face

例 他才不干修车这种活呢,怕掉价。

► He doesn't want to do car repair work for fear of losing face.

D

掉链子 diào liàn zi

◆ break down; have problems; go wrong; make mistakes

例 这台电脑平时用得挺好的，可今天关键时刻就掉链子了，总是死机。

▶ This computer normally works very well, but it broke down at a crucial moment today, and shut down frequently.

跌份 diē fèn

◆ lower yourself, lose face

例 一个教授怎么能做出这种事来，真是跌份。

▶ How can a professor do such a thing? How embarrassing!

丁克 dīng kè

◆ DINK; a short term for dual income, no kids

例 近年来在大城市里出现了不少丁克家庭。

▶ In recent years, many DINK families have come forth in big cities.

钉子户 dīng zi hù

◆ recalcitrant; person or household who refuses to move and bargains for a very high compensation when their land is requisitioned for a construction project

例 这个地方要拆迁，别人都搬走了，只有他坚决不搬家，成了钉子户。

▶ All the residents moved from the old houses which will be pulled down soon except him. He became the hardest recalcitrant.

顶 dǐng

◆ support or agree; a term used on the Internet, especially in BBS

例 我顶。

► I support.

东东 dōng dōng

◆ thing; a term used on the Internet

例 听说那家小店里有不少好玩的东东,还不去淘点儿?

► I heard that there are many interesting things in that small shop. Would you go to buy some?

动漫 dòng màn

◆ cartoon, animated film

例 他最喜欢日本的动漫,是个动漫迷。

► He likes Japanese cartoons the most, and is a cartoon fan.

豆腐渣工程 dòu fǔ zhā gōng chéng

◆ jerry-built projects

例 新盖的楼房,没过一年就塌了,这就是最典型的豆腐渣工程。

► The new building fell down within one year. That's a typical jerry-built project.

读图时代 dú tú shí dài

◆ graphic reading time

例 "读图时代"的到来一度成为中国文化界的热点话题之一,并令许多人深感忧虑。

▶ The arrival of "graphic reading time" has become one of the hot topics in cultural circles of China and has caused great worries for many people.

D

肚皮舞 dù pí wǔ

◆ belly dance

例 肚皮舞在京城悄然流行起来,不少健身房都开设了这一健身项目。

▶ Belly dancing has quietly become popular in Beijing. Many gyms have begun offering this as a fitness regimen.

断背(臂)duàn bèi (bì)

◆ brokeback mountain

例 《断背山》在赢得美国金球奖后,"断背"一词便成为"同性恋"的代名词。

▶ After the film *Brokeback Mountain* got the Golden Globe Award in the United States, the word "brokeback" has become a synonym for "gay".

对路子 duì lù zi

◆ 1. meet the requirement; satisfy the need; be just right

例 我们应该多作市场调查,生产出更多对路子的产品。

▶ We should do more market research, and produce more products to satisfy the need.

◆ 2. be to one's liking; suit one

例 他的这个想法与当前的形势有些不对路子。

▶ His idea doesn't suit the current situation.

多媒体 duō méi tǐ

◆ multimedia

例 这是一个学习英语的多媒体软件,是对英语学习的一次革命。

▶ This is a multimedia English learning software. It's a revolution to the English study.

D

夺金 duó jīn

◆ win the gold metal

例 在男子自由体操项目上,他具有夺金的实力。

▶ In the gymnastic competition, he has the strength to win the gold metal.

E

E

恶补 è bǔ

◆ cram; do remedial work very hard in one's study; study hard to improve one's knowledge

例 全国各地的选手们都在恶补奥运知识,加紧备战奥运火炬手的选拔。

► Players from all over the country are cramming for the Olympic Games and getting ready to attend the selection for torch holders of the Olympic Games.

恶搞 è gǎo

◆ mischief; spoof; make fun of; play a joke on someone or something

例 达·芬奇著名的油画《蒙娜丽莎》遭人恶搞。

► De Vinci's famous painting "Mona Lisa" was spoofed by someone.

耳朵根子软 ěr duo gēn zi ruǎn

◆ soft ear; a person who is easily swayed by other's words

例 他这个人什么都好,就是耳朵根子软,没有个准主意。

► He is a good person, but he's got a soft ear, and never makes up his mind.

二 èr

◆ idiot; stupid, silly, but lovely

例 你不觉得这人问这个问题有点二吗?

▶ Don't you think the question he asked is somewhat silly?

二手车 èr shǒu chē

◆ second-hand car

例 最近二手车市场很火。

▶ Recently, the market for second-hand cars is very hot.

二手房 èr shǒu fáng

◆ second-hand house

例 为了上班方便,他在城里买了一套二手房。

▶ To be closer to work, he bought a second-hand apartment in the city.

二手香 èr shǒu xiāng

◆ second-hand fragrance; a perfume that is so strong that makes other people around feel uncomfortable

例 在公共场合,二手香就像二手烟一样惹人生厌。

▶ In public situations, second-hand fragrance is as loathsome as second-hand cigarette smoke.

二手烟 èr shǒu yān

◆ second-hand cigarette smoke, passive smoke

例 政府出台了在公共场所禁止吸烟的规定,以保护公众免受二手烟的影响。

▶ The government has enacted a regulation restricting smoking in public places to protect the public from the dangers of second-hand cigarette smoke.

F

发憷 fā chù

◆ feel timid and uneasy, become nervous; be keyed up

例 她一见到领导，就发憷，不知道该说什么。

▶ She feels timid and uneasy as soon as she meets her boss, and doesn't know what to say.

发了 fā le

◆ make a fortune; get rich

例 他这两年做生意发了，又买房子又买车。

▶ He's made a fortune in the past two years, so he bought a house and a car.

发毛 fā máo

◆ be afraid of, be terrified, be scared, get gooseflesh

例 《尖叫》这部恐怖电影让我看得直发毛。

▶ The horror movie *Screaming* made me get gooseflesh.

发烧友 fā shāo yǒu

◆ enthusiastic fan; fanatic

例 他是一个音乐发烧友，他的音响设备是最先进的。

▶ He is a music fanatic. His sound system is the most advanced.

发帖子 fā tiě zi

◆ send a message

例 这件事一经披露,就有不少网友发贴子表达自己对此事的看法。

► Once this thing was revealed, many net friends sent messages expressing their views on it.

反腐倡廉 fǎn fǔ chàng lián

F

◆ combat corruption and build a clean government

例 今年政府继续加大反腐倡廉的力度,搞好党风建设。

► This year the government will continue to stress on combating corruption and building a clean government, and will construct the work style of the party well.

反恐 fǎn kǒng

◆ anti- terrorism

例 两国领导人希望进一步加强两国在反恐方面的合作。

► Leaders of both countries hope to further strengthen their cooperation in anti-terrorism efforts.

反弹 fǎn tán

◆ rebound, rally

例 股市在经过几天的下跌后,今天出现强烈反弹。

► The stock market, after a few days' fall, rebounded fiercely today.

返券 fǎn quàn

◆ gift coupon returned

例 调查发现,大多数顾客喜欢商场打折,而不喜欢返券。

▶ According to investigations, most customers like department stores to give discounts, but don't like gift coupons returned.

犯傻 fàn shǎ

◆ 1. act foolishly, stupid

例 你别犯傻了,这种坏天气,他才不会来呢。

▶ Don't be stupid. He won't come in such a bad weather.

◆ 2. stare blankly; be in a daze

例 你别站在那儿犯傻了,快过来帮我一下。

▶ Don't stand there acting foolishly. Come quickly over here to help me.

饭局 fàn jú

◆ banquet, feast, dinner party

例 今天晚上他有饭局,不知道什么时候才到家呢。

▶ He'll have a banquet tonight. I don't know when he will come back home.

防暴 fáng bào

◆ anti-riot

例 政府强调要不断提高防范、处置恐怖袭击事件的能力和水平,扎扎实实做好奥运安保、反恐防暴工作。

▶ The government emphasized gradual improvement of abilities and skills guarding against and handling terrorists' attacks, and to provide excellent safety services and riot control for the Olympics.

房贷 fáng dài

◆ housing loan

例 他每个月都要还房贷,所以日子过得有些紧。

► He pays his housing loan every month, so he is short of money.

房价 fáng jià

◆ housing price

例 现在的房价越来越高,每平米已经卖到一万多块钱了。

► The price of houses is getting higher and higher now. It has cost more than ten thousand yuan per square meter now.

房奴 fáng nú

◆ house slave; someone who must work very hard to earn enough money to pay their mortgage

例 房价的飙升造就了一批"房奴"。

► The rising price of houses has created a large number of "house slaves".

房爷 fáng yé

◆ house lender; someone who makes money by renting houses to people

例 他买了几套房子,准备当"房爷"了。

► He bought several apartments and plans to be "a house lender".

非物质文化遗产 fēi wù zhì wén huà yí chǎn

◆ non-material cultural heritage

例 中国的昆曲已被联合国教科文组织认定为非物质文化遗产。

▶ The Kunqu Opera of China has been recognized as the non-material cultural heritage by UNESCO.

费改税 fèi gǎi shuì

◆ charge to tax; It refers to the substitution of administrative charge with tax payment

例 酝酿十年之久的燃油"费改税"问题再度引起了人们的关注。

▶ The "charge to tax" issue which has been under consideration for ten years has once again caught people's attention.

分流 fēn liú

◆ (in economic restructuring) reposition of redundant personnel

例 他们努力做好企业分流人员的安置工作。

▶ They are trying diligently to finalize the repositioning of redundant personnel of the corporation.

粉领 fěn lǐng

◆ pink-collar worker; pink collar

例 大学毕业后,几经周折,小刘最后还是选择了做一名粉领。

▶ After graduation from college, Xiao Liu underwent several setbacks and finally decided to be a pink-collar worker.

粉丝 fěn sī

◆ fans

例 这个明星的粉丝男女老少都有。

▶ The star's fans include men and women, old and young.

封杀 fēng shā

◆ strangle; smother

例 这部电视剧因为格调低下刚刚播出就遭到封杀。

► This TV show was strangled soon after it was broadcast because of its low moral quality.

风险投资 fēng xiǎn tóu zī

◆ venture investment

例 2006 年,中国已经取代英国成为全球风险投资第二大目标国。

► In 2006, China replaced Britain as the second largest target country of global venture investment.

峰会 fēng huì

◆ summit (meeting)

例 这次峰会的主要议题,就是如何面对日益严重的全球变暖问题。

► The main topic of discussion for this summit is how to face the problem of increasingly severe global warming.

扶贫工程 fú pín gōng chéng

◆ anti-poverty project, help-the-poor project; project of aiding a poverty-stricken area

例 "中国健康扶贫工程"是继"希望工程"后的一项国家级扶贫项目。

► The Anti-Poverty Project of Health in China is a national level project after the Hope Project.

福娃 fú wá

◆ Fuwa, Beijing Olympic Mascot

例 奥运福娃由贝贝(鱼)、晶晶(大熊猫)、妮妮(燕子)、欢欢(圣火)、迎迎(藏羚羊)五个形象组成。

▶ **Fuwa, the Beijing Olympic mascots, are composed of 5 figures, including Beibei (the fish), Jingjing (the panda), Huanhuan (the Olympic flame), Yingying (the Tibetan Antelope), and Nini (the swallow).**

F

负翁 fù wēng

◆ debtor

It has the same pronunciation as "moneybags" in Chinese, but is opposite in meaning. So it is ironic to call a debtor "Fuweng" in Chinese.

例 很多有房有车的年轻人都是"负翁",他们最担心的就是失业。失业了拿什么去还贷款呢?

▶ **A lot of young people with houses and cars are debtors. What they worry most is losing their jobs. If they lose their jobs, how can they return all the loans used to buy the houses and cars to the bank?**

G

盖了帽 gài le mào

◆ extremely good; the best; excellent

例 这个球打得真是盖了帽，引起看台上观众的一片欢呼。

▶ That play was extremely good. It caused a sudden roar of cheers from the audience in the stands.

概念车 gài niàn chē

◆ concept car

例 在刚开幕的车展上，人们看到不少漂亮的概念车。这些车通常是世界各大汽车公司显示其科技实力和设计观念的主要方式。

▶ At the recent car exhibition, people saw many beautiful concept cars. These cars are usually used to display the scientific and technological strength and ideas of the car companies' designs.

肝儿颤 gānr chàn

◆ have a shaken liver; tremble with fear; be terrified, be scared

例 我学习太差，一听说要考试就肝儿颤。

▶ I am scared stiff on hearing taking examinations.

赶趟儿 gǎn tàngr

◆ have time for, be in time for

例 离电影开演的时间还有一小时，咱们现在去还赶趟儿。

▶ The film will be on in an hour. We can be in time for it if we go right now.

高产低耗 gāo chǎn dī hào

◆ high production and low consumption

例 这个地区去年的经济实现了“高产低耗”。

► This region has realized “high yield and low consumption” in economy last year.

高开低走 gāo kāi dī zǒu

G

◆ high open, low close

例 过去只在少数高档楼盘的销售中才用的“高开低走”营销策略,如今已经被开发商普遍采用。

► The marketing strategy of “high open and low close” used in the sales of a few top-grade builings before has been widely adopted by developers today.

高考移民 gāo kǎo yí mín

◆ Immigrants for college entrance exam

It refers to the students who move to a province where is easier to get a high scores and be enrolled by colleges and universities.

例 高考移民客观上带到了移入城市的房价的提升。

► Objectively, immigrants aiming at national entrance examinations to colleges and universities increase the price of real estate.

搞定 gǎo dìng

◆ settle, fix; make sure

例 这件事情今天必须搞定,不能再拖了。

► This thing must be settled today. It can't be postponed any longer.

搞笑 gǎo xiào

◆ (words or actions) meant to amuse someone or to cause laughter

例 许多人喜欢看憨豆先生的电影，因为他很搞笑。

► Many people like to watch Mr. Bean's movies because he is good at amusing people.

割肉 gē ròu

◆ sell (stock, national debt, commodity) at a lower price than one buys

例 不少炒股的人都体会过割肉的滋味。

► Many stock investors have experienced selling stocks at a lower price than they paid.

跟风 gēn fēng

◆ to follow suit or trends; do as others do

例 自从《人体使用手册》卖火了之后，在书店，你会发现跟风出版了很多雷同的书。

► After the book *Body Usage Handbook* sells well as a bestseller, you can find many similar books following suit in bookstores.

跟帖 gēn tiě

◆ follow up

例 1. 看到他在网上发表的观点后，有不少人跟帖表示支持。

► After reading his opinions published on the net, many people followed up to support him.

例 2. 他的博客有上百万的点击率和数万个跟帖，非常热闹。

► His blog has gotten over one million click-through rates and thousands of follow ups. It is very hot.

G

跟着感觉走 gēn zhe gǎn jué zǒu

◆ follow one's intuition

例 这个工作非同一般,你可要严肃对待,不能跟着感觉走。

▶ This work is different from ordinary one (unusual). You should treat it seriously, and you can't just follow your intuition.

狗仔队 gǒu zǎi duì

G

◆ snapper, photographer

例 为了摆脱狗仔队,这对当红影星秘密地去国外结婚了。

▶ In order to break away from the snappers, the famous movie star couple went abroad to get married secretly.

够劲儿 gòu jìnr

◆ 1. heavy, strong (in taste, strength, etc.), strenuous

例 这个箱子可够劲儿,你肯定搬不动。

▶ This suitcase is pretty heavy. You definitely can't move it.

◆ 2. almost too much to cope with, difficult

例 想三天就把这本书都啃下来,够劲儿。

▶ It's almost too much to finish this book in three days. (It's too difficult to finish this book in three days.)

股民 gǔ mín

◆ person who buys and sells stocks

例 中国有成千上万的股民每天关注着股票市场的涨跌。

▶ There are thousands of stock investors in China. They pay great attention to the rise and fall of the stock index everyday.

股市 gǔ shì

◆ stock market

例 股市有风险，投资需谨慎。

▶ The stock market is risky. Please be cautious if you invest.

骨感 gǔ gǎn

◆ bony, skinny

例 为了让自己具有骨感美，她拼命节食。

▶ She tries very hard to stay on a diet in order to make herself look skinny.

骨灰级 gǔ huī jí

◆ prelude grade, hardcore, top grade

例 登上这些山峰的人基本都属于骨灰级玩家。

▶ Those who have climbed to the top of these mountains are almost considered to be “prelude grade” players.

关系户 guān xì hù

◆ closely-related units

例 他今天晚上要宴请公司的那些关系户。

▶ He will treat his company’s clients to dinner tonight.

灌水 guàn shuǐ

◆ to fill web pages with content or articles; write articles on BBS of a website

例 欢迎大家来到“英语之声”论坛灌水。

G

► Welcome to the forum (BBS) "Voice of English". Please submit your articles on BBS.

光污染 guāng wū rǎn

◆ light pollution (undesirable illumination)

例 中国科学院一位专家说,尽管建筑物的玻璃幕墙造成的光污染已经开始引起人们注意,但其他类型的光污染却仍然鲜为人知。

► An expert at the Chinese Academy of Sciences said that the light pollution caused by glass walls of buildings have already caught people's attention, but other kinds of light pollution are little known.

国脚 guó jiǎo

◆ players on the national soccer team

例 在国外踢球的中国国脚逐渐多起来,这其实是一件好事。

► There are more and more Chinese players on the national soccer team playing abroad in foreign clubs, which is actually a good thing.

过 guò

◆ overdo something; go too far

例 今天你做的这件事有点过了,你对他又不了解,干吗对他那么热情啊?

► You went too far today. You don't know him well. Why did you treat him so warmly?

过劳模 guò láo mó

◆ better than a labor model

It refers to one who works over 10 hours a day and usually has no rest days, doesn't have enough sleep and has infrequent meals. It is also used to refer to mid-level, middle class and core workers who have high education, high income and high position.

例 据调查结果显示，白领往往是“过劳模”的主要人群。

► According to the result of one survey, white-collar workers make up the main group of “better than a labor model”.

过劳死 guò láo sǐ

◆ overstrained death

例 近年来中年人过劳死的事件频频见诸报端，引起了人们的注意。

► In recent years, news about overstrained death of middle-aged people has frequently appeared in newspapers, catching people's attention.

H

哈韩族 hā hán zú

◆ young people who love Korean pop songs, TV dramas and dress style

例 在大学里有相当一批人是哈韩族，他们狂热地追捧韩国流行的影视剧明星及其穿着打扮。

▶ There are quite a number of people in colleges and universities who love Korean pop songs or TV dramas. They are crazy about Korean TV dramas, movie stars and their dressing style.

哈日族 hā rì zú

◆ young people who love Japanese pop songs, TV dramas and dress style

例 这些哈日族只是追捧日本流行的一些表象的东西，并不真正了解日本社会。

▶ Young people who love Japanese pop songs or TV darams only love the presentation of these things. They don't really understand Japanese society.

海 hǎi

◆ 1. plenty, extremely large

例 1. 我听说你喝酒可是海量，谁也不是你的对手。有这回事吗？

▶ I heard that you are a heavy drinker, and nobody is your equal, really?

例 2. 今天前去买奥运门票的人海了去了，那队排得老远老远的，有几百米。

► Today the number of people buying tickets of the Olympic Games was extremely large. The line was quite long, over several hundred meters.

◆ 2. willy-nilly, without a goal

例 我不知把那本书放在哪儿了，结果只能海找一通。

► I didn't know where I put the book, as a result I had to look for it willy-nilly.

海带 hǎi dài

H

◆ a homophonic phrase for 海待, referring to those who come back after study abroad and have difficulty finding employment

例 他没有选择回国，因为担心自己会变成"海带"。

► He didn't choose to return to his homeland for fear that he would not find a job.

海龟 hǎi guī

◆ a homophonic phrase for 海归, referring to Chinese returning from overseas, mainly those who come back after study abroad

例 这场秋季招聘会的规模很大，吸引了众多刚毕业的大学生，还有不少"海龟"参加。

► The employment fair in the autumn season is large in scale, such that it has attracted many new graduates, and many who have come back from study abroad.

海选 hǎi xuǎn

◆ extensive audition, large-scale audition, massive audition, select from an extremely large range

例 这十个人就是从全国奥运舵手选拔赛中海选出来的。

► These ten people were selected from an extensive audition of national Olympic steersmen trials.

韩剧 hán jù

◆ Korean TV drama

例 她特别喜欢看韩剧，每天晚上都要看到夜里 12 点。

► She loves to watch Korean TV dramas very much, and watches until 12 o'clock every evening.

韩流 hán liú

◆ Korean wave; fashion or trend from South Korea, a homophonic phrase of 寒流

例 这两年"韩流"盛行，无论是韩国时尚的音乐、影视还是服装都在中国受到人们的青睐。

► In the past two years, the Korean wave is very strong. Regardless if it's Korean modern music, TV dramas and movies or clothes, all are very popular among people in China.

航展 háng zhǎn

◆ aerospace exhibition; aviation expo

例 刚开幕的航展吸引了无数青少年前来参观。

► The newly opened Aerospace Exhibition has attracted numerous young people to come and visit.

喝高了 hē gāo le

◆ drink too much alcohol; get drunk

例 看样子他今天是喝高了，说起话来没完没了。

▶ It seems that he drank too much alcohol today for he kept talking all the time.

和谐社会 hé xié shè huì

◆ harmonious society

例 和谐社会的灵魂就是人的和谐。

▶ The soul of harmonious society is the harmony of the people.

贺岁片 hè suì piàn

◆ film shown on New Year occasions, New Year greeting film

例 冯小刚的新片《天下无贼》一公映便获得观众的好评，这是他推出的第四部贺岁片。

▶ As soon as Feng Xiaogang's new movie *A World without Thieves* was shown to the public, it was well received by audiences. That is the fourth New Year greeting film he produced.

黑 hēi

◆ 1. greedy, avaricious, evil-minded, crafty

例 那个老板太黑，干一天活连一分钱都不给。

▶ That boss is too greedy. He didn't pay a penny to one who worked for him for a day.

◆ 2. extort, extract; do something unlawful, illegal

例 那家伙真不地道，黑了我一笔钱跑了。

▶ That guy is too bad. He extorted some money from me and disappeared.

黑车 hēi chē

◆ Illegal taxi, taxi without licence

例 地铁外边停的多数都是黑车，千万别坐。

► Most of the cars parking outside the subways are illegal taxis. Don't take them.

黑客 hēi kè

◆ hacker

例 昨天这家公司的网站遭黑客袭击，导致所有数据丢失。

► Yesterday the company's website was attacked by hackers and all the data was lost.

H

黑色收入 hēi sè shōu rù

◆ black income

例 他被查出上百万元的黑色收入。

► He was discovered to have over one million yuan black income.

黑哨 hēi shào

◆ black whistle; a metaphor for an unfair decision of a judge (referee) who is partial or who has been bribed

例 在足球联赛中吹黑哨的事情频繁发生。

► In football league matches, black whistle events happen frequently.

黑五类 hēi wǔ lèi

◆ the five black elements: black sesame, black rice, black dates, black soybeans, black fungus

例 黑五类食品营养价值高，被认为是健康食品，如今已经越来越受到人们的欢迎。

▶ The food of five black elements contains high nutrition and is considered to be very healthy food. It is becoming ever more popular today.

忽悠 hū you

◆ 1. rock, sway, flicker

例 别拿这个东西在我眼前忽悠,看着让人眼晕。

▶ Don't rock it in front of my eyes. It makes me dizzy.

◆ 2. confuse and corrupt people's minds, agitate one to believe

例 他经不起推销员的再三忽悠,掏钱买了几盒保健品,结果服用后非但没效果,反而拉肚子住进了医院。

▶ He couldn't stand the repeated agitation of the salesman and bought several boxes of the health care products. After taking them, he found no results at all, but went to hospital with a case of diarrhea.

胡子工程 hú zi gōng chéng

◆ bearded project; a metaphor for long-drawn-out projects; a project which takes so long that young workers become bearded

例 市政府正在清理一批"胡子工程"。

▶ The municipal government is cleaning up a group of "bearded projects".

话痨 huà láo

◆ one who is talkative, who won't stop talking

例 像他这样的话痨如果不去作销售,真是有点可惜了。

▶ It's really a pity for a talkative person like him if he doesn't work as a salesman.

H

皇粮 huáng liáng

◆ emperor's grains; a metaphor for state-paid salary

例 在政府部门工作的人都是吃皇粮的，工资虽然不是很高，但工作稳定，不用担心会突然失业。

▶ People working in government organs live on emperor's grains. Although their salary is not high, their work is stable and they don't worry about losing their jobs suddenly.

H

黄昏恋 huáng hūn liàn

◆ twilight love; falling in love at an elder age

例 1. 一位八旬老人勇敢地谈起了黄昏恋，与对方见面三次就结婚了。

▶ An eighty-year-old man is brave enough to fall in love. He only met his mate three times before they were married.

例 2. 如今黄昏恋已经广泛地被人们所接受。

▶ Today, twilight love is widely accepted by most people.

黄金周 huáng jīn zhōu

◆ Golden Week

It refers to the seven days off during the Spring Festival, Labor Day, and National Day.

例 在"十一黄金周里"人们扎堆儿出游，机票和火车票都得提早预订。

▶ During the golden week of October 1, people go traveling all together. Plane and train tickets have to be booked in advance.

黄了 huáng le

◆ come to naught; go through without result

例 这件事再这么拖下去就黄了。

▶ This thing will come to naught if it is postponed like this any longer.

黄牛党 huáng niú dǎng

◆ ticket scalper

例 春节期间各大商场返券促销吸引了大量消费者，同时也招来了商场"黄牛党"，他们靠倒券代购一天能赚上千元。

▶ During the Spring Festival, sales promotions involving gift coupons in all large department stores have attracted many consumers, and ticket scalpers as well. They can make more than one thousand yuan a day by speculating gift coupons.

灰领 huī lǐng

◆ gray collar; gray-collar worker; workers in maintenance service, such as auto mechanics, electrical repairmen, etc.

例 现在大学生找工作难，不少人选择去当灰领。其实，如今灰领工人的工资一点不比白领低。

▶ Now it's difficult for a college graduate to find a job. A lot of people decide to work at a gray collar job. Actually, a gray-collar worker's salary is not lower than that of a white collar worker nowadays.

灰色收入 huī sè shōu rù

◆ extra income

例 他每月能挣不少钱，除了工资以外，还有一些灰色收入。

▶ He earns a lot of money every month. Besides his salary, he's also got some extra income.

回头客 huí tóu kè

◆ returning customer

It refers to customers who return to a place once or more often. Also a metaphor for a place that has built up a prosperous business, has a reputation for good quality goods at cheap prices and attracts customers back.

例 这家饭馆的生意可好了,来这里吃饭的有不少人都是回头客。

▶ **This small restaurant's business is very good. Many who come to dine here are returning customers.**

H

会来事儿 huì lái shìr

◆ know how to cater to someone's tastes; good at getting along with others; butter someone up

例 他这人聪明,还特别会来事儿,把那位领导哄得很高兴。

▶ **He is clever and knows how to get along with others. He made that leader very happy.**

婚外恋 hūn wài liàn

◆ extramarital love

例 婚外恋是导致他们离婚的主要原因。

▶ **Extramarital love is the main reason for their divorce.**

J

唧唧歪歪 jī jī wāi wāi

◆ twitter

例 我不喜欢他唧唧歪歪的样子，一点儿不像男子汉。

▶ I don't like him because he twitters and talks endlessly while he speaks, not like a man.

基金 jī jīn

◆ stock fund

例 今年股市行情好，他买的基金也让他挣了不少钱。

▶ The stock market is good this year. He has earned a lot of money through buying and selling stock funds.

基民 jī mín

◆ person who buys and sells stock funds, speculator in the stock market, investor

例 股市的几次暴跌，给新基民闷头一击。

▶ Several sudden stock market declines gave many new investors a head-on blow, leaving them with a great loss.

集资房 jí zī fáng

◆ houses built with the funds collected by the buyers

例 他们单位准备今年建集资房。

▶ Their unit is going to construct houses with the funds collected by the buyers this year.

绩优股 jì yōu gǔ

◆ blue chip stock

例 绩优股成为了今年的市场热点之一。但是这并不意味着随便买入一只绩优股就能赚钱。

▶ Blue chip stocks have become one of the hot spots of the market this year, but it doesn't mean that one can make money by buying blue chip stocks randomly.

◆ It also refers to a single man with high educational background and good work.

例 他在我们公司被认为是"绩优股",有许多女孩追他。

▶ He is regarded as the "blue chip stock" in our company and many girls chase after him.

家庭暴力 jiā tíng bào lì

◆ family violence

例 家庭暴力是困扰国内外妇女的重要问题之一,在家庭暴力中通常受到伤害最多的是妇女。

▶ Family violence is a significant problem which troubles many women at home and abroad. Women are always victims of the family violence.

家庭影院 jiā tíng yǐng yuàn

◆ home theater; home audio and video systems with high quality sound effects and screen pictures

例 许多人在自己的家里配备了家庭影院。

▶ Many people equipped themselves with a home theater at their home.

例 家庭影院让您在家就可以享受到在影院的震撼力。

▶ Home theater allows you to enjoy the effect of a cinema.

家政服务 jiā zhèng fú wù

◆ household management service

例 家政服务已成为一个备受社会关注的新兴行业。

▶ Household management service has become a new socially concerning industry.

假唱 jiǎ chàng

◆ lip-synch

例 新修订的《营业性演出管理条例》明确规定了对于假唱的处罚方法。

▶ The newly revised Rules for the Implementation of the Regulation on the Administration of Commercial Performances clearly regulates the methods of penalty for lip-synching.

假冒伪劣 jiǎ mào wěi liè

◆ fake and inferior; counterfeit and shoddy products

例 他没有想到自己花钱买回来的名牌皮鞋竟是假冒伪劣产品，还没穿几天就坏了。

▶ He didn't expect that the famous-brand leather shoes he bought were fake and inferior ones. They were broken in only a few days.

价格听证会 jià gé tīng zhèng huì

◆ public price hearings

例 近两年举行的 30 多次价格听证会，议题主要集中在水电气、交通、景点门票等关系人民群众切身利益的方面。

▶ In more than 30 public price hearings held in the past two years, the topics for discussion have mainly focused on charges for water, electricity and gas, traffic tolls, admission tickets for scenic spots, and other fields related closely to people's vital interests.

坚挺 jiān tǐng

◆ robust, solid and strong, often used in reference to a currency that is stable and keeps rising on the international exchange rate

例 1. 罗杰斯认为最坚挺的货币就是人民币。

▶ Rogers thinks the most solid and strong currency is Renminbi (RMB).

例 2. 这种产品可以使乳房变得坚挺、饱满、秀美。

▶ This product can make the breasts protuberant, plump and beautiful.

减负 jiǎn fù

◆ lighten the burden, reduce study load

例 政府下令给学生减负，可奇怪的是学生的学习负担却越减越重。

▶ The government ordered a reduction of students' study load, but strangely the students' load was increased rather than reduced.

交强险 jiāo qiáng xiǎn

◆ Compulsory Traffic Accident Liability Insurance for Motor Vehicles

例 一份交强险只是最初级的保障，对于经常上路的司机来说，其实并不够用。

▶ A Compulsory Traffic Accident Liability Insurance for Motor Vehicles is only the most fundamental insurance. For drivers who always work on roads, it's in fact not enough.

叫板 jiào bǎn

◆ challenge; ask for trouble; pick a quarrel

例 你才学几天呀，就敢跟我叫板，我今天就让你知道我的厉害。

▶ How long have you dared to challenge me? I'll give you a lesson today.

叫停 jiào tíng

◆ ask to stop; call stop

例 今天有两家工厂因环保问题被叫停，并限时整改。

▶ Today two factories were called to stop due to problems related to environmental protection, and were asked to reform and consolidate in a limited time.

较真儿 jiào jiào zhēnr

◆ serious

例 这件事没什么大不了的，你们俩就别较真儿了。

▶ This is a trifling thing. You two shouldn't take it so seriously.

接轨 jiē guǐ

◆ 1. connect the rails

例 敦煌铁路不久将要与青藏铁路接轨。

▶ Dunhuang railway will soon connect their rails with the Qinghai-Tibet railway.

◆ 2. get onto the track; integrate

例 中国的经济要与世界接轨，还有许多工作要做。

▶ As our economy becomes global, there will be lots of work to do.

节能降耗 jié néng jiàng hào

◆ save energy and reduce consumption; energy efficiency and consumption reduction

例 节能降耗是中国经济社会发展的必然选择，并已成为中国经济减轻能源压力的重要途径。

► Saving energy and reducing consumption is an inevitable choice for Chinese social economic development, and it has become an important way to reduce the pressures of energy on the Chinese economy.

J

节能型 jié néng xíng

◆ energy-saving

例 在抓住市场机遇、提升现代化管理水平的同时，这家公司一直致力于节能型企业的建设和节能型产品的开发，坚持走可持续发展之路。

► While pursuing market opportunities and improving modernized administration standards, this company has devoted itself to the construction of energy-saving enterprises and the use of energy-saving products, and has insisted on walking the road of sustainable development.

节约型社会 jié yuē xíng shè huì

◆ conservation-oriented society

例 2004 年初，中国政府正式提出建设节约型社会，使资源得到节约使用，环境得到保护，人民生活更加文明、健康、科学，经济与社会持续发展。

► At the beginning of 2004, the Chinese government formally declared plans to build a conservation-oriented society in order to use resources economically, protect the environment and make the lives of people more civilized, healthier and scientific, as well as to promote continuous development of the economy and society.

金领 jīn lǐng

◆ gold collar, gold-collar worker

It refers to the high-level professionals, such as engineers, lawyers, analysts, programmers, etc.

例 随着信息和高科技产业的兴起，越来越多的金领族们出现了，"金领"一词也充分体现出他们在公司的地位。

► Along with the increasing prevalence of information and high-technology industries, more and more gold-collar workers appeared. The word "gold collar" also fully reflects their role in a company.

J

禁捕 jìn bǔ

◆ be prohibited from fishing; prohibit fishing

例 松花江从今起进入禁捕期。

► Songhua River has entered its prohibited fishing period from now on.

禁放 jìn fàng

◆ (of fireworks and firecrackers) be prohibited

例 北京曾经禁放烟花爆竹十余年。

► Fireworks and firecrackers have been prohibited in Beijing for more then ten years.

禁改限 jìn gǎi xiàn

◆ prohibition changed into limitation

例 由于禁改限政策的出台，2006 年春节，烟花爆竹的生意一下红火起来。

► Since the policy changing prohibition into limitation was announced, sales of fireworks and firecrackers for the Spring Festival have boomed.

经济适用房 jīng jì shì yòng fáng

◆ economic houses

例 今年将再建一批经济适用房，以适应中低收入家庭的需要。

► Another group of economic houses will be built this year to meet the requirements of middle and low-income families.

精装修 jīng zhuāng xiū

◆ delicate internal decoration

例 一段时间以来，精装修的商品房成为社会关注的热点。

► For a period of time, delicate internal decoration for commodity houses has become a hot spot concerning the society.

绝了 jué le

◆ unique, excellent, brilliant

例 你怎么想出这个主意来的，真是绝了。

► How did you come up with this idea? It's brilliant.

K

卡丁车 kǎ dīng chē

◆ go-cart, a mini Formula one-style racing car

例 卡丁车赛是世界流行的赛车运动,同时也是一项极具魅力的户外休闲运动。

► The go-cart racing competition is a world popular car racing sport. It is also a very attractive outdoor sport for entertainment.

卡拉 OK kǎ lā OK

◆ karaoke

例 卡拉 OK 是青年人喜爱的娱乐项目之一。

► Karaoke is one of the entertainments loved by young people.

开盘 kāi pán

◆ opening quotation (on the exchange)

例 开盘后股指快速冲高。

► After the opening quotation, the stock index soared.

◆ begin to sell

例 1. 在 8 月即将开盘的项目里,小户型房屋仍处于稀缺状态。

► In projects going to open quotation in August, there is still a shortage of small-room apartments.

例 2. 北京市内新楼开盘的均价已超过每平方米一万元。

► The average price of opening quotation of new buildings in Beijing exceeds ten thousand yuan per square meter.

侃 kǎn

◆ chat idly, tattle

例 他这人特别能侃，跟他在一起，你绝对不会感到寂寞。

▶ He is extremely talkative. You'll never feel lonely being with him.

砍价 kǎn jià

◆ bargain

例 在自由市场买东西，你一定得砍价，否则就会吃亏。

▶ While buying things at free markets, you must bargain. Otherwise, you'll pay too much.

看病难 kàn bìng nán

◆ hard to see a doctor

例 在这个城市，"看病难"的问题一直没有得到很好解决。

▶ In this city, the difficulty in seeing a doctor hasn't been solved.

考博 kǎo bó

◆ take the entrance examination for a doctor's degree

例 1.她准备今年夏天考博。

▶ She is going to take the entrance examination for a doctor's degree this summer.

例 2.这家网站有大量的考博资讯。

▶ There is much information on taking the entrance examination for a doctor's degree on this website.

考级 kǎo jí

◆ grade examination

例 如今社会上有各种各样的考级，如英语考级、音乐考级、计算机考级等等。

▶ There are various grade examinations for students, such as English grade examination, music grade examination, computer grade examination and so on.

考研 kǎo yán

◆ take the post graduate school entrance examination

例 为了逃避就业的压力，许多大学毕业生选择考研。

▶ To avoid the pressure of employment, many college graduates choose to take the post graduate school entrance examination.

靠 kào

◆ fuck, damn (swearword); used to express one's anger or upset

例 靠，这次考试又考砸了。

▶ Damn, I didn't do well again in this exam.

靠谱 kào pǔ

◆ reasonable; sound

例 听说汽车要降价，你觉得这事靠谱吗？

▶ I heard the price of cars would drop. Do you think it's reasonable?

科博会 kē bó huì

◆ High-tech Expo

例 科博会是一个促销新产品和新技术的好平台。

▶ The High-tech Expo is a good platform for promoting new

products and technology.

科技奥运 kē jì ào yùn

◆ Scientific Olympics

例 北京奥运会火炬处处闪现科技之光，体现了“科技奥运”的理念。

▶ The torch designed for the Beijing Olympic Games reflects the light of technology and expresses the concept of a “Scientific Olympics”.

科学发展观 kē xué fā zhǎn guān

◆ Scientific Concept of Development

例 科学发展观就是全面、协调和可持续的发展观。

▶ Scientific Concept of Developmnet is an overall, coordinated and sustainable development view.

可持续发展 kě chí xù fā zhǎn

◆ sustainable development

例 我们必须认真实施可持续发展战略，把环境保护和生态建设放到更加重要的位置。

▶ We must implement the sustainable development strategy seriously, and consider environmental protection and ecosystem construction as a higher priority.

啃老族 kěn lǎo zú

◆ NEET(not in education, employment or training)

例 随着就业压力增大，越来越多成年的独生子女加入“啃老族”的队伍。

▶ Due to an increase in unemployment rates, more and more adult single-children join the ranks of NEET.

空巢 kōng cháo

◆ empty nest

例 中国传统的三代同堂家庭越来越少了，取而代之的是更多的空巢家庭。

▶ There are fewer traditional large families with three generations living together in China and more empty-nest families.

空巢老人 kōng cháo lǎo rén

◆ empty nester, empty-nest senior citizens; parents whose children have grown up and moved away from homes

例 据调查，大部分空巢老人不愿住进敬老院。

▶ According to a survey, most empty-nest and lonely senior citizens don't want to live in old folk's homes.

孔子学院 kǒng zǐ xué yuàn

◆ the Confucius Institute

例 许多外国人在孔子学院学习汉语和关于中国的知识。

▶ Many foreigners learn Chinese language and culture in the Confucius Institute.

恐龙 kǒng lóng

◆ (derogatory term first used on the Internet) a dinosaur; a metaphor for an ugly girl

K

例 她怎么能是美女啊，分明是恐龙嘛。

► She's not a beauty. She is a dinosaur.

抠门儿 kōu ménr

◆ stingy, closefisted, penny-pinching, miserly

例 他是一个抠门儿的老头，从不会请人吃饭的。

► He is a penny-pinching old man. He never treats anyone.

口水仗 kǒu shuǐ zhàng

◆ quarrel

例 他们两人从不动手，天天在办公室里打口水仗。

► These two people never fight, but quarrel at the office everday.

酷 kù

◆ cool; used to show that you admire or approve of something because it is fashionable, attractive and often different

例 你瞧他这身打扮多酷啊！

► Look at his clothes. How cool he is!

酷毙了 kù bì le

◆ very or extremely cool; the coolest, the best

例 你设计的这个广告酷毙了，没人能比得上。

► The advertisement you designed is the coolest. Nobody comes up to it (can compete with you).

快餐 kuài cān

◆ fast food

例 如今想吃快餐很容易,大街上到处都能找到快餐店。

► It's very easy to have fast food now. You can find fast-food restaurants on every street.

快男 kuài nán

◆ abbreviation for 快乐男声(**kuài lè nán shēng**)

Happy Boy is the title of a television program. Now it is used as an abbreviation referring to the boys performing on the show.

例 参加完2007年"快乐男声"选秀节目的快男们绝大多数很快就被人们遗忘了。

► The participants for the 2007 *Happy Boy* TV show are easily forgotten by people.

宽带 kuān dài

◆ broadband

例 这个小区的人都可以使用宽带上网。

► People in this community can get on the Internet through broadband.

K

L

垃圾股 lā jī gǔ

◆ junk stock

例 那家公司的股票是垃圾股，便宜，却没有人会买。

► That company's stock is junk. It's cheap, but nobody buys.

拉动内需 lā dòng nèi xū

◆ spur domestic demand

例 中国实行的"黄金周"长假制度确实对拉动内需起到了一定作用。

► The implementation of Golden Week spurs domestic demand.

来劲 lái jìn

◆ 1. get excited, become alive; become full of energy; inspire

例 他天生就是个运动员的料，一上赛场就来劲。

► He was a born athlete, getting excited as soon as he competes with others.

◆ 2. make trouble; find fault with

例 你别来劲，我正跟别人说话呢。

► Don't make trouble. I'm talking with someone else.

蓝牙 lán yá

◆ "Bluetooth" technology; a short distance wireless communication technology

例 这一款是蓝牙手机，可以无线传输信息。

▶ This is a Bluetooth mobile phone. It can transmit information in a wireless way.

烂尾楼 làn wěi lóu

◆ unfinished building

例 这个开发商由于遭遇金融危机，导致资金链断裂，致使他开发的一处楼盘成为烂尾楼。

▶ This developer suffered from a financial crisis causing his capital chain to break off. Now the building is unfinished.

老冒儿 lǎo màor

◆ hick, an ignorant or ill-informed person

例 你真是个老冒儿，都什么年代了，连手机都不会用！

▶ You're really a hick. You don't even know how to use a mobile phone.

老三样 lǎo sān yàng

◆ three most common things in a category

例 1. 过去买车，人们都爱买那老三样，它们的质量信得过。

▶ In the past when people bought cars, they preferred to buy three brands: Santana, Jetta and Citroen, which have creditable qualities.

例 2. 每年体检都离不开老三样。

▶ Annual physical check-up can not get rid of (always includes) three things: eyesight, weight and height.

冷处理 lěng chǔ lǐ

◆ cold treatment; a metaphor for giving something a cooling-off period before addressing it, tackling a matter after all parties concerned have cooled down

例 这件事情由于双方争执得很厉害,只好先冷处理一下,过两天再讨论。

► Since both sides hold on their positions on this matter, it'd be better to have a cold treatment first and discuss it two days later.

廉租房 lián zū fáng

◆ cheap rent housing

例 中国推出廉租房,只出租给城镇居民中最低收入者,这类房不可以出售。

► The cheap rent housing in China is only for rent, not for sale. It is rented to residents in cities and towns who have the lowest income.

两会 liǎng huì

◆ two conferences referring to the National People's Congress (NPC) and Chinese People's Political Consultative Conference (CPPCC)

例 "两会"期间,各国记者云集北京,争相报道。

► Correspondents from all over the world came to Beijing to report the news of the NPC and CPPCC during the conferences.

亮点 liàng diǎn

◆ bright spot; a metaphor for (someone or something) to be attractive and eye-catching

例 1. 鸟巢将是北京奥运会的一个亮点。

▶ The "Bird's Nest" (The National Stadium) will be a bright spot of the Beijing Olympic Games.

例 2. 新修订的义务教育法呈现六大亮点，首次明确义务教育免收学杂费。

▶ The newly revised compulsory education law has six bright spots. It declares for the first time that the compulsory education is free of tuition fees.

亮晶晶 liàng jīng jīng

◆ glittering, glistening, sparkling, shining; a combination of the first names of two Chinese famous divers Tian Liang and Guo Jingjing

例 据报道,"亮晶晶"一同到成都出席昨晚的晚会。

▶ According to the report, Tian Liang and Guo Jingjing went to Chengdu together to attend the evening party yesterday.

L

靓 liàng

◆ beautiful, fashionable, good-looking

例 这款手机可够靓的。

▶ How fashionable the mobile phone is.

靓女 liàng nǚ

◆ beautiful woman, pretty girl

例 他只顾看靓女了,哪有心思和我们聊天。

▶ He's only focused on looking at beautiful women. Why would he chat with us?

靓汤 liàng tāng

◆ delicious soup

例 有人说广东的“老火靓汤”看起来很讲究，其实很容易做。

▶ Some say that the delicious “laohuo” soup of Guangdong Province is very delicate and complicated in making, but actually it's quite simple.

靓仔 liàng zǎi

◆ handsome young man

例 别看他现在老了，想当年他也是个靓仔哪。

▶ He's old now, but he used to be a handsome young man in his prime.

猎头 liè tóu

L

◆ headhunting; look for senior talented people in all kinds of fields

例 猎头公司是一个专门为客户寻找和推荐所需人才的服务公司。

▶ A headhunting agency is a service company which engages in looking for and recommending talented people to its agents.

临时抱佛脚 lín shí bào fó jiǎo

◆ make effort at the last moment

例 你最好早些复习，别等要考试了才临时抱佛脚。

▶ You'd better review your lessons earlier, and don't make your effort at the last minute when the exam is approaching.

另类 lìng lèi

◆ a different, special, completely new or fashionable type or trend

例 他的新作被人称为另类小说，颇有些与众不同。

▶ His new work is regarded as a novel of a special and completely new type. It's quite different from the others.

流动人口 liú dòng rén kǒu

◆ floating or transient population

例 流动人口数量的急剧增加，对于促进城乡经济的发展、加强区域间的科技文化交流、繁荣和活跃市场具有非常重要的作用。

► The transient population increases very quickly. It plays a very important role in improving the development of urban and rural economies, enhancing the scientific and cultural exchange between regions, and making the markets more lively and prosperous.

流口水 liú kǒu shuǐ

◆ mouth watering; long for something

例 这一桌美味让人看了直流口水。

► The delicious food on the table makes one's mouth water when seeing it.

流浪猫 liú làng māo

◆ abandoned cat, stray cat

例 她收养了三只流浪猫。

► She has adopted three stray cats.

例 瞧你这脏兮兮的样子，你这是从哪里来？搞得自己跟流浪猫似的。

► Look at your dirty face. Where did you go? You look like a stray cat.

流氓软件 liú máng ruǎn jiàn

◆ rascal software, malware, spy ware

例 几天前网络行业协会公布了十大流氓软件的名单，这些软件大多是强制安装，而且不容易卸载。

L

▶ Several days ago, the Network Industry Association issued a list of ten rascal softwares. Most of these programs are automatically installed, and are difficult to remove.

流通股 liú tōng gǔ

◆ circulation stock

例 在上市公司的股票中，一般可将其分为流通股和非流通股两大类。可以在股票市场进行交易的股票就是流通股。

▶ Stocks coming into the market are usually divided into two kinds: circulation stock and noncirculation stock. The one which can be traded in the stock market is circulation stock.

留守儿童 liú shǒu ér tóng

◆ rear children; a child left to live with his or her grandparents or relatives while his or her parents go to work in another place or province

例 这些孩子的父母外出打工去了,他们留在家里,成了留守儿童。

▶ These children are left with relatives while their parents go out to work in another city. They become the rear children.

龙头 lóng tóu

◆ leader; the leading things

例 这是一个以防爆产品为龙头产业的多元化企业集团。

▶ This is a diverse corporate group with explosion resistant devices as its leading product line.

龙头企业 lóng tóu qǐ yè

◆ leading company

例 青海省六家企业成为农业产业化国家重点龙头企业。

▶ Six companies in Qinghai Province became the key national leading companies of agricultural industrialization.

隆胸 lóng xiōng

◆ breast augmentation

例 据专家透露,接受隆胸的女人,以 20 多岁的居多,不过,也有 60 多岁的老龄妇女。

▶ Experts revealed that women who received breast augmentation are mostly over the age of 20. But some are older women over the age of 60.

楼盘 lóu pán

◆ building

例 1:全国范围内各大城市新楼盘的信息都能在这家网站上查询。

▶ Information on new buildings in cities all over the country can be found on this website.

例 2:开发商推出什么类型的楼盘,最主要的还是由供需市场决定。

▶ What types of buildings are developed are mainly decided by the market of supply and demand.

楼市 lóu shì

◆ building market, property market

例 据有关数据显示,杭州楼市下半年供应量为 500 万平方米。

▶ Evidence shows that the supply of buildings in Hangzhou in the latter half of the year is five million square meters.

露脐装 lòu qí zhuāng

◆ bare midriff

例 露脐装因其大胆前卫、张扬青春活力而成为许多时尚女性青睐的夏日时装。

▶ Bare midriff has become the summer style favored by many fashionable women showing their boldness and vitality.

驴友 lǘ yǒu

◆ backpacker buddy; hiking fellows; those who travel together

例 自助游作为一种时髦的旅游方式,广泛受到驴友们的青睐。

▶ Self-help travelling as a modern way of travel wins the favor of most backpacking buddies.

绿色食品 lǜ sè shí pǐn

L

◆ green food; organic foods without chemical additives

例 人们越来越钟爱绿色食品。

▶ People like the green food more and more.

乱搭 luàn dā

◆ 1. miss-matched (clothes)

例 今年穿衣流行乱搭。

▶ Dressing in a miss-matched way is in fashion this year.

◆ 2. illegal construction

例 本市近日拆除乱搭乱建房屋 1100 间。

▶ This city has torn down 1,100 illegally built houses recently.

论坛 lùn tán

◆ forum

例 1. 据了解，很多实力雄厚的著名台商纷纷表示将会参加这次论坛。

论坛的主题是“加强两岸农业合作，实现两岸农业互利双赢”。

▶ It's said that many powerful and famous businessmen from Taiwan would attend this forum. The topic of the forum is "Strengthening cooperation on agriculture between Mainland China and Taiwan to achieve double wins and mutual benefits on agriculture for both sides".

例 2. 网上这个论坛人气很旺，来灌水的人也很多。

▶ This online forum is very hot. Many people leave messages on it.

裸奔 luǒ bēn

◆ nude run

例 昨天下午一名男子在街头裸奔，引来路人驻足观看。

▶ Yesterday afternoon, a nude man ran in the street causing passers-by to stop and watch.

落马 luò mǎ

◆ fall off the horse; a metaphor for a government official losing his or her post for committing a crime or for illegal activities

例 近年来，不少高官因贪污腐败纷纷落马。

▶ In recent years, many high-ranking officials have fallen from their horses one after another because of corruption.

M

码长城 mǎ cháng chéng

◆ play mahjong

例 退休后，许多老年人每天都聚在一起码长城。

▶ After retirement, many old people gather together to play mahjong every day.

埋(买)单 mái(mǎi) dān

◆ pay the bill

例 今天说好了，我埋单，谁也不许跟我抢。

▶ I'll pay the bill today. No one will argue with (grab it from) me.

卖座 mài zuò

◆ (of a theater, cinema, etc.) draw large audiences; (of a movie, etc.) be a box-office success; (of a restaurant, club, etc.) attract many customers

例 在香港十大卖座影片中，周星驰的影片就占了三部，《功夫》、《少林足球》和《审死官》。

▶ Of the ten most successful box-office films in Hong Kong, Stephen Chow's has three: *Kung Fu Hustle*, *Shaolin Soccer*, and *Justice, My Foot*!

盲流 máng liú

◆ blind influx

It refers to people, mainly laborers, who are aimlessly flowing from rural areas or small towns into large cities.

例 在北京、上海、广州等大城市，盲流人数呈逐年上升趋势。

▶ In big cities of Beijing, Shanghai, and Guangzhou, numbers accounting for blind influx go up year after year.

猫 māo

◆ 1. modem

例 现在上网都用宽带，不再使用“猫”了。

▶ Now people use broadband to access the Internet, and no longer use a modem.

◆ 2. hide

例 一见有人走过来，他急忙找个地方猫起来了。

▶ As soon as he saw someone coming, he quickly found a place to hide.

M

猫腻 māo nì

◆ illegal deal, underhanded activity; also say 猫儿腻 (**māor nì**)

例 这个比赛结果太出人意料了，总让人感觉里面有猫腻。

▶ The result of this match was so unexpected that it made people think there was an illegal deal involved.

毛坯房 máo pī fáng

◆ rough housing, raw housing

例 政府出台新规定，禁止销售未经装修的毛坯房。

▶ The government made a new regulation prohibiting selling rough housing.

没劲 méi jìn

◆ 1. uninteresting, boring

例 这个电影没劲透了,看了一半就有不少人退场。

▶ This film is very boring. Many people left in the middle of it.

◆ 2. (of person) good-for-nothing, not very promising, disappointing

例 你这人真没劲,连这点小事都不敢做,怎么能办得了大事呢?

▶ You are really good-for-nothing. You dare not do even small things. How can you do anything big?

没门儿 méi ménr

◆ no way, can't do it

例 别指望着我能借你钱,没门儿。你上次借的钱还没还呢!

▶ Don't expect me to lend you money. No way. You haven't returned the money you borrowed from me last time.

M

没脾气 méi pí qi

◆ can not lose one's temper, helpless, can hardly find a way out, mild tempered

例 1. 这件事你坚持了很久可到头来还得听他的,弄得你最后也没脾气了。

▶ You have to listen to him for it in the end. It makes you totally helpless at last.

例 2. 他生再大的气,可一见到他老婆就立刻没脾气了。

▶ No matter how angry he is, he can not lose his temper once he sees his wife.

没谱 méi pǔ

◆ 1. unsure, unrealistic, be irrelevant, unsettled

例 你先别着急,这事现在还没谱呢。

▶ Don't worry now. It hasn't been settled yet.

◆ 2. have no idea, not know

例 他这个人到底怎么样,我可没谱,小王应该最了解他。

▶ I don't know how he is. Xiao Wang should know him better than I.

没戏 méi xì

◆ have no hope; hopeless, impossible

例 如果他这点儿还不来,你就别等了,没戏了。

▶ If he hasn't come by now, you should not wait for him any longer. There's no hope that he will come today.

没辙 méi zhé

◆ have no other way out, have no solution

例 他们不愿意降价,我也没辙。

▶ They don't want to lower the price. I can do nothing about it. (I have no other way out about it.)

没治 méi zhì

◆ 1. hopeless, helpless

例 他这人就是这个脾气,真是没治了。没人能说服得了他。

▶ That's hopeless. He is that kind of person. Nobody can persuade him.

◆ 2. extremely great

例 这台晚会真是没治了,太棒了。

▶ This evening's performance was extremely great.

美眉 měi méi

◆ MM; an abbreviation for beautiful girls

例 香港被誉为"购物天堂",时尚的美眉大多愿意去那里购物。

► Hong Kong is recognized as a shopping paradise. Most fashionable beautiful girls like to go shopping there.

猛男 měng nán

◆ valiant man, strong man, brave man

例 他每天都泡在健身房里,一心想做一个像施瓦辛格那样的肌肉猛男。

► He stays in the gym all day every day, hoping to be a strong muscular man like Arnold Schwarzenegger.

面 miàn

◆ weak, lax, slow

例 他做事特别面。

► He does things very slowly and is incapable of doing things well.

名人效应 míng rén xiào yìng

◆ celebrity charm, celebrity effect

例 名人效应是商业广告中最常用也是最为有效的手段之一。借助名人的知名度和影响力,达到广告宣传目的。

► Celebrity charm is the most commonly used and one of the most effective means in commercial advertisement. With the help of the name-recognition and influence of the celebrity, one can achieve their promotional purpose.

名嘴 míng zuǐ

◆ famous pundit (of television anchor, host or hostess)

例 这台晚会汇集了央视不少名嘴参加。

► This evening party has invited many famous pundits of CCTV stations to attend.

摩的 mó dí

◆ motorbike taxi

例 执法人员当场查处一名正在违章运营的摩的司机。

► A tipstaff caught an illegal motorbike taxi driver on the spot.

M

N

脑残 nǎo cán

◆ mentally retarded, addle minded; also used in the cartoon field to refer to characters of cartoons drawn with idiot looks

例 看完这个影片,你一定会脑残的。

► After seeing this movie, you will become addle minded.

闹心 nào xīn

◆ be worried or disturbed, be vexed

例 把音乐关掉！大热天的听这种音乐闹心不闹心?

► Turn off the music! Don't you feel disturbed listening to this kind of music on such a hot day?

能耗 néng hào

◆ energy consumption

例 中国首次将能耗指标列入国家发展目标。

► China has created an index of energy consumption for a national development goal for the first time.

黏糊 nián hu

◆ sticky, glutinous

例 他再三叮嘱你多放点水,不要把粥熬得太黏糊了。

► He warned you repeatedly to put more water in the porridge and not to make it too sticky.

◆ slow in action, in low spirits

例 别看他平时很黏糊,有事的时候他比谁都利索。

▶ He seems to be an indecisive person, but he is more neatly decisive than anyone when he is truly needed.

◆ like to be together

例 你们俩别老黏糊在一起,还是找点事做吧。

▶ You two should find some work to do instead of just always staying together.

鸟巢 niǎo cháo

◆ Bird's Nest; It refers to the National Stadium which looks like a big bird's nest.

例 "鸟巢"位于北京奥林匹克公园内。

▶ The Bird's Nest is located in the Beijing Olympic Games Park.

N

牛 niú

◆ proud, arrogant, self-important

例 他总是显得特别牛,其实没什么真本事。

▶ He always looks very proud, but in fact he has no real ability.

牛市 niú shì

◆ bull market

例 进入 2007 来以来,中国股市一直呈牛市,多数玩股票的人都挣钱了。

▶ Since 2007, the stock market of China has turned into a bull market, and most people who buy and sell stocks have made money.

农民工 nóng mín gōng

◆ farm worker, migrant worker, rural labor

例 在这个城市里,拖欠农民工工资的事情时有发生。

► In this city, pay for farm workers is sometimes delayed.

暖冬 nuǎn dōng

◆ warm winter

例 暖冬把北京的秋天变长了。

► Warm winter makes the autumn of Beijing longer.

O

欧 III 标准 ōu sān biāo zhǔn

◆ European emission standards

例 现在市场上销售的新车都要符合欧 III 标准。

► New cars for sale on the market must meet European emission standard III.

偶像派 ǒu xiàng pài

◆ idol type with good looks

例 1. 他年轻俊朗的外表使他成为偶像派的代表。

► His young and cool appearance makes him representative of the idol type.

例 2. 这是偶像派与实力派的一场较量。

► This is a challenge between idol type and talent type.

呕像 ǒu xiàng

◆ a disgusting person who makes you want to vomit, a homophone of 偶像, but with a contrast meaning

例 你真是我的“呕像”啊，瞧瞧你这身打扮，怎么能出门呢？

► You are really my “disgusting idol”. How dare you go out dressed like this?

P

拍砖 pāi zhuān

◆ hit somebody with a stone; a metaphor for criticizing somebody on blog or BBS

例 如果没有了拍砖人，网上无疑将是一潭死水，毫无生气。

► If there's no one criticizing another on the BBS, the website will no doubt be a pond of dead water, not lively at all.

派对 pài duì

◆ 1. party

例 昨天晚上，她的生日派对有许多明星参加，也吸引了众多媒体的目光。

► Many famous stars attended her birthday party yesterday evening, and attracted the attention of the media.

◆ 2. make pairs; matchmaking

例 在 12 名征婚者中，只有两对派对成功。

► Among the twelve people looking for marriage partners only four made pairs successfully.

盘活 pán huó

◆ make alive, rejuvenate

例 在实行体制改革后，一些老企业被盘活了。

► After carrying out system reform, some old enterprises have been rejuvenated.

泡吧 pào bā

◆ Indulge oneself for a long time in bars (wine bars or Internet bars)

例 如今喜欢泡吧的人多了,酒吧的生意也就格外红火。

► Nowadays, increasing numbers of people love to stay in bars, which make booming business for the bars.

泡沫经济 pào mò jīng jì

◆ bubble economy

例 写字楼租金出现泡沫经济破灭以来的最大涨幅。

► The rent of office buildings got its biggest increase since the bubble economy burst.

泡汤 pào tāng

◆ fall flat, fall through (of plans), fail, be done for, be unsuccessful, come to nothing; be fruitless

例 这事你得抓紧办,搞不好就要泡汤了。

► You'd better do it quickly, otherwise, it might fall flat.

陪聊 péi liáo

◆ accompany someone to chat

例 她找了个陪聊的工作,服务对象多为老人。

► She found a job to accompany people to chat. Most of her customers are old people.

喷饭 pēn fàn

◆ spurt out food with laughter; something which is so funny and ridiculous that makes someone spew out their food (at meals)

例 你最好别再往下说了,否则我就忍不住要喷饭了。

► You'd better not go on talking. Otherwise, I can't help spurting out food with laughter.

碰瓷儿 pèng cír

◆ porcelain-crashing; intentionally throwing oneself onto or in front of a moving car to get compensation

The term employs the word "porcelain" because it's fragile and could be costly.

例 他专门找出租车司机碰瓷儿。

► He only looks for taxi drivers to do porcelain crashing.

疲软 pí ruǎn

◆ 1. (of a person) fatigued and weak

例 手术后,他感到浑身疲软,站不起来。

► After the operation, he felt fatigued and weak, unable to stand up.

◆ 2. weak, slumping, sluggish (in market)

P

例 手机市场疲软的一个主要原因是同类产品过多。

► The main reason for the sluggish market of mobile phones is the overabundance of similar products.

飘红 piāo hóng

◆ enjoy positive red figures

例 最近数码相机的销售业绩全线飘红。

► The sales of digital cameras are enjoying positive red figures.

票房 piào fáng

◆ box office (of a cinema, theater, stadium)

例 这部影片获得去年全美票房冠军。

▶ This film had the highest box office returns in the United States last year.

品位 pǐn wèi

◆ taste

例 她很有品位,买的衣物都与众不同。

▶ She is one with high taste in fashion. The clothes she buys are all unique.

平价医院 píng jià yī yuàn

◆ fair-price hospital

例 北京市首家平价医院——上地医院开业。

▶ The first fair-price hospital in Beijing, Shangdi Hospital, opened.

平台 píng tái

◆ platform, opportunity

例 公司提供给他一个施展才华的平台。

▶ The company provided an opportunity for him to give full play to his talents.

Q

齐活 qí huó

◆ be done, be over or finished

例 1. 等我把这个做完,就齐活了。

▶ I'll be done when I finish this one.

起哄 qǐ hòng

◆ become a spectator; "crash" an event; encourage trouble

例 看见别人举办婚礼,他就跑过去看热闹,跟着起哄。

▶ Seeing others holding a wedding ceremony, he would run over to see what't going on.

起腻 qǐ nì

◆ bother someone; pester, nag

例 别跟我这儿起腻,不做完功课不能出去玩。

▶ Don't pester me. You can't go playing outside until you finish your homework.

汽车美容 qì chē měi róng

◆ car beauty, car care

例 这是第一个专业作汽车美容和保养的网站。

▶ This is the first professional car beauty and care (maintenance) website.

潜规则 qián guī zé

◆ hidden rules, unwritten rules

例 人们对影视圈内的潜规则的态度不尽相同。

► People take different attitudes toward the unwritten rules of the movie and television industry.

强 qiáng

◆ excellent, good

例 哦,他可真强,这次考试数学又考了满分。

► Oh, he is really great. He got a full mark in maths again in this examination.

强强联合 qiáng qiáng lián hé

◆ make joint effort through integration of excellent enterprises

例 两个集团都是本行业的领军企业,强强联合之后,无疑会大大提升竞争力。

► Both groups are leading enterprises of their industries. After making joint effort through integration, they will no doubt greatly increase their competition strength.

强势 qiáng shì

◆ strong force, driving force

例 人们希望中国队能继续保持强势体育项目上的领先优势。

► People hope that Chinese teams will continue to maintain the leading advantage in strong force sports events.

例 中国经济保持强势增长。

► Chinese economy keeps a driving-force increase.

抢眼 qiǎng yǎn

◆ eye-catching, conspicuous

例 这款新车在车展上最为抢眼。

► The new car is the most eye-catching of the car exhibition.

亲和力 qīn hé lì

◆ affinity

例 一个人的亲和力往往取决于他/她的性格。

► One's affinity usually depends on his or her personality.

青蛙 qīng wā

◆ frog; bad-looking man (net langnage)

例 他虽然是个"青蛙",但正直,幽默,很讨美眉喜欢。

► Althrough he is a"frog", he is honest and humorous. Many girls like him.

情商 qíng shāng

◆ E.Q. (emotional quotient)

例 情商决定一个人的成败。

► One's E.Q decides the success and failure of a person.

全球变暖 quán qiú biàn nuǎn

◆ global warming

例 全球变暖会导致冰川融化、海平面上升以及灾害天气增多。

► Global warming can cause glaciers to melt, sea levels to rise and make disastrous weather happen frequently.

拳头产品 quán tóu chǎn pǐn

◆ competitive products, knock-out products, blockbuster

例 这款手机是这家公司的拳头产品。

▶ This mobile phone is the company's knock-out product.

R

热炒 rè chǎo

◆ promote frequently in media, increase in value due to popularity

例 1. 她的新书正在各大报纸上热炒。

► Her new book is promoted frequently in all the newspapers.

例 2. 一套几元的奥运纪念邮票热炒至 100 元。

► One set of Olympic commemorative stamps for several yuan has increased in value up to 100 yuan.

热点 rè diǎn

◆ hot spot

例 伊拉克一直是全球的新闻热点。

► Iraq has been the hot spot for world news.

热线 rè xiàn

◆ hot line

例 奥运服务热线即将开通。

► The Olympic service hot line is going to be opened.

热销 rè xiāo

◆ (of goods) in great demand; sell like hot cakes; hot sale

例 保健品一直是市场最热销的产品之一。

► Health care products are among the hottest products on the market.

人脉 rén mài

◆ having many personal relationships; popular

例 他成功的另一个最重要的因素就是他的人脉资源相当丰富。

► Another important key for his success is that he has very rich resources in personal relationships.

人气 rén qì

◆ popularity

例 周杰伦在青年人中人气最旺。

► Zhou Jielun has the highest popularity among young people.

肉 ròu

◆ not crisp, mushy

例 这西瓜瓤儿太肉了,一点都不好吃。

► The watermelon is not crisp. It tastes bad.

◆ (of a person) slow in getting things done; not frank; not straightforward

例 他做事特别肉,让人看着就着急。

► He does things very slowly, and makes you worried if you see him.

软广告 ruǎn guǎng gào

◆ soft ads; a type of advertisement in the form of a newspaper or magazine article or short TV show; It tells life stories of clients enjoying certain products so as to create a good image of the product.

例 软广告充斥着各大媒体。

► There are many soft ads found throughout all types of media.

软拒 ruǎn jù

◆ soft excuse, refuse in a reasonable way

例 他的采访请求遭到公司的软拒。

▶ His request for an interview resulted in a soft excuse.

软肋 ruǎn lèi

◆ weak point, Achilles' heel

例 她的话一针见血，直戳他的软肋，他能不生气吗？

▶ Her words hit the nail on the head and stabbed right to his weak point. How could he not get angry?

软实力 ruǎn shí lì

◆ soft power

例 提高"软实力"将不可避免地触及到许多复杂的问题，如体制、观念等方面的改革等。

▶ Improving soft power will inevitably touch many complicated problems, such as reform of systems, concepts and so on.

软着陆 ruǎn zhuó lù

◆ soft landing

例 中国经济实现软着陆。

▶ The Chinese economy had a soft landing.

弱势群体 ruò shì qún tǐ

◆ weak group, socially vulnerable group

例 关注弱势群体应成为社会公正的重要内容之一。

▶ **Paying attention to the more vulnerable population should become one of the main contents of social justice.**

弱智 ruò zhì

◆ weak-minded, mentally deficient, stupid

例 这道题出得有些弱智。

▶ This is a stupid question.

S

三高 sān gāo

◆ three highs

1. high degree, high income and high position

例 据调查，在大城市里，"三高（高学历、高收入、高职位）"单身男女青年的人数在不断增多。

▶ According to one survey, the number of three-high single young men and women in big cities is increasing.

2. high blood pressure, high blood fat (hyperlipidemia) and high blood sugar (hyperglycemia)

例 "三高（高血压、高血脂、高血糖）"人群要做到早预防、早发现、早治疗。

▶ The three-high risk group should practice early prevention, seek early discovery and early treatment.

三农 sān nóng

◆ Three-agriculture, three problems of agriculture; It refers to agriculture, rural areas (countryside), and farmers

例 中国作为一个农业大国，"三农"问题关系到国民素质、经济发展，关系到社会稳定、国家富强。

▶ In China, as a big agricultural country, the three-agricultural problem is concerned with national quality, economic development, social stability and national prosperity.

三栖明星 sān qī míng xīng

◆ tri-circle star; the actor or actress popular in film, television, and song circles

例 他是中国大陆最受欢迎的三栖明星之一。

▶ He is one of the most popular tri-circle stars in Mainland China.

杀价 shā jià

◆ force down the price, chop down the price

例 在旅游景点买东西，你必须学会杀价，否则就会挨宰。

▶ While buying things at tourist attractions, you must learn how to chop down the price. Otherwise, you will pay too much.

杀熟 shā shú

◆ a metaphor for cheating one's acquaintances

例 做生意最怕遇到杀熟的人。

▶ People who do business are afraid of meeting one who cheats acquaintances.

沙尘暴 shā chén bào

◆ sandstorm

例 入春以来，北京遭遇了好几次沙尘暴。

▶ Since spring, Beijing has suffered several sandstorms.

沙发 shā fā

S

◆ 1. sofa

例 这是真皮沙发。

▶ This is a genuine leather sofa.

◆ 2. sofa grabbing, originating from the pronunciation of "so fast", a term used in network referring to the first one who sends a message in reply to a blog host

例 她是徐静蕾的粉丝，每天都要上她的博客抢沙发，今天她终于抢到了。

► She is a Xu Jinglei fan. She sees her blog and tries to grab the sofa everyday. Today, she finally succeeded in sofa grabbing.

晒工资 shài gōng zī

◆ to put one's salary amount on the net

例 许多人认为晒工资是一件好事，它可以增加薪水的透明度，促进行业发展。

► Many people think that it's a good thing to put one's salary amount on the net. It can increase the transparence of the salary and accelerate the development of the industry.

煽情 shān qíng

◆ 1. arouse one's enthusiasm, fervor

例 他的节目以煽情著称。

► His program is known for arousing people's enthusiasm.

◆ 2. flirt

例 他总忘不了跟女孩子煽情，这是他最大的毛病。

► He can not avoid flirting with girls. That is his biggest weak point.

S

闪 shǎn

◆ 1. dodge; get out of the way

例 他一遇到困难就闪。

► As soon as he meets with difficulties, he dodges.

◆ 2. trick, fool

例 他们把我们给闪了，说好了今天都来这里，他们却没来。

▶ They tricked us. We had agreed to come here today, but they didn't show up.

闪存 shǎn cún

◆ flash ROM, flash card, flash memory, U disc

例 他买了一个新闪存。

▶ He bought a new flash card.

闪婚 shǎn hūn

◆ lightning marriage, instant marriage

It refers to a couple who get married as quickly as lightning after knowing each other for a very short time

例 时下,"闪婚"成了未婚年轻人的时尚,闪电般地相识,闪电般地擦出爱情火花,闪电般地结婚。

▶ Nowadays "lightning marriage" has become a fashion for some young people—lightning acquaintance, lightning love sparks, and lightning marriage.

闪居 shǎn jū

◆ cohabit with an unfamiliar person shortly after meeting him or her

例 传统的爱情、婚姻,在"闪居"的撞击下,已是支离破碎。

▶ Traditional love and marriage have been shattered under the impact of cohabiting with an unfamiliar person shortly after the meeting.

例 据介绍,闪居者以 80 后的年轻人居多。

▶ According to introduction, cohabitants are mostly young people born in the 1980s.

商海 shāng hǎi

◆ business field, commercial circle

例 他在商海打拼了10年，积累了丰富的经验。

► He has been doing business for ten years, and gained rich experience.

商品房 shāng pǐn fáng

◆ commercial residential building

例 商品房的价格一升再升，没有丝毫降的意思。

► The price of commercial residential buildings continually rises, and doesn't give any signs of dropping.

商业贿赂 shāng yè huì lù

◆ commercial bribery

例 在一些行业和领域，商业贿赂在一定程度上已成为"潜规则"。

► In some trades and fields, commercial bribery has become a "hidden rule" to a certain extent.

商战 shāng zhàn

S

◆ trade war, price war

例 这本书采用了章回小说的形式，写的是真实的激烈商战，所涉及的人物都是用的真名。

► This book, in the form of chapters of a novel, is about real and fierce trade wars. All the characters' names are real.

上火 shàng huǒ

◆ 1.suffer from excessive internal heat (with such symptoms as constipation, conjunctivitis, and inflammation of the nasal and oral cavities)

例 他牙疼,一定是上火了。

▶ He had a toothache. He must suffer from an excessive internal heat.

2.flare up angrily

例 孩子不听话,你能不上火吗?

▶ The child didn't listen to you. Why didn't you flare up?

上扬 shàng yáng

◆ rise, go up

例 股指大幅上扬,报收于 4900 点。

▶ The stock index went up greatly and closed at 4,900 points.

上座率 shàng zuò lǜ

◆ box-office rate

例 这部电影上映一周,表现不俗,上座率超七成。

▶ This film has had a good return after showing in theaters for a week. The box-office rate is over 70 percent.

烧钱 shāo qián

◆ burn money; a metaphor for spending money quickly

例 目前情况下,国内视频网站烧钱的局面仍将持续至少三年。

▶ Under present circumstances, the situation of money burning on domestic video frequency websites will continue for at least three years.

蛇头 shé tóu

◆ snakehead; It refers to the heads or key figures in organizations that smuggle illegal immigrants.

例 国际刑警抓住一个蛇头。

▶ **The international police have arrested a snakehead.**

神 shén

◆ supernatural, magical, amazing

例 这件事太神了,没人会相信。

▶ **This thing is too amazing. Nobody will believe it.**

神六 shén liù

◆ shenzhou-6 spacecraft

例 中央电视台将于周三现场直播"神六"的发射。

▶ **CCTV will broadcast the launch of Shenzhou-6 spacecraft live on Wednesday.**

审美疲劳 shěn měi pí láo

◆ aesthetic tiredness, tiredness in aesthetics

例 1. "审美疲劳"成了婚姻的杀手。

▶ **"Aesthetic tiredness" becomes a killer of marriages.**

例 2. 他设计的这几套图书封面太过雷同了,会让读者产生"审美疲劳"。

▶ **The covers he designed for these books are quite similar to each other, which may cause aesthetic tiredness among readers.**

S

生态旅游 shēng tài lǚ yóu

◆ ecotourism

例 生态旅游使一些地区脱贫致富。

▶ **Ecotourism allows some regions to shake off poverty and attain prosperity.**

十一五规划 shí yī wǔ guī huà

◆ the 11th five-year plan

The Five-Year Plan for National Economic and Social Development; The five-year plan for 2006-2010 is called the 11th Five-Year Development Guidelines

例 继续深化规划体制改革,是“十一五规划”工作的一项重要任务。

▶ Continuing to deepen reforms of the planning system is an important task of the 11th Five-Year Plan.

食品安全 shí pǐn ān quán

◆ food security (safety)

例 食品安全问题一直是人们所关注的焦点。

▶ Foof security is always a question of concern for people.

事儿 shìr

◆ 1. way, means, measure

例 这个问题总不解决也不是个事儿,还是赶紧想办法吧。

▶ This problem can't be put off unsolved like this. You'd better think of a way to solve it quickly.

◆ 2. meddlesome, troublesome, overly concerned

例 你怎么这么事儿啊,人家干得不是挺好的嘛。

▶ How troublesome you are! I have done pretty well on my own.

S

视觉污染 shì jué wū rǎn

◆ visual pollution

例 这个广告不仅影响市容市貌,而且造成严重的“视觉污染”。

▶ This advertisement not only gives a bad image to the city's appearance, but also causes severe visual pollution.

视频聊天 shì pín liáo tiān

◆ video chat; chat through video frequency

例 喜爱网上聊天的人如今又多了一种聊天方式——视频聊天。

► Those who love to chat online now have one more way to communicate–video chatting.

试婚 shì hūn

◆ trial marriage

例 在年轻人中流行的试婚做法让多数家长无法接受。

► Most parents are unable to accept the trial marriages so prevalent among young people today.

瘦身 shòu shēn

◆ get one's body thinner; slim down

例 最近人们发现,成功瘦身的她比以前漂亮了不少。

► Recently, people discovered that she has become more beautiful than before after she slimmed down.

◆ a metaphor for streamlining administration structure or downsizing an organization

例 裁员成了各大企业瘦身的首选方式。

► Laying off employees has become the primary way for companies to slim down.

梳理 shū lǐ

◆ put something in order; disentangle (a confused situation), readjust

例 他想好好梳理一下自己的思路,写成一份报告。

► He wants to put his ideas in good order and write a report.

数字化 shù zì huà

◆ digitalized

例 不久,图书出版业将进入数字化时代。

► The book publishing industry will enter the digital era soon.

数字家庭 shù zì jiā tíng

◆ digital home, digital household

This means a fully automated residence. China is trying to help more and more families have access to Internet services and other home appliances powered by digital technology

例 数字家庭是信息产业向消费发展的一个分支，它侧重技术的应用，强调信息化。

► Digital home is a branch of development from the information industry to consumer. It emphasizes application of technology, stressing information.

刷卡 shuā kǎ

◆ pay by credit card

例 她喜欢刷卡买东西,又方便又快捷。

► She likes to buy things by credit card. It's convenient and fast.

S

耍大牌 shuǎ dà pái

◆ put on air, make a show of authority, throw one's weight about; be overbearing, vaunt one's celebrity or power

例 有一媒体指责他耍大牌,不按时回国家队训练。

► One report criticized him for putting on airs (vaunting his celebrity) and not coming back to train with the national team.

衰 shuāi

◆ bad luck, be down on one's luck

例 最近真衰，这么点小事我都没办成！

► What a bad luck! I even failed to do such a little thing.

帅呆 shuài dāi

◆ (of males' appearance) very handsome, outstanding

例 他在电影中的形象简直帅呆了，难怪那么多人喜欢看这部电影呢！

► His image in the film is very handsome. No wonder so many people love to see that film.

涮 shuàn

◆ trick, fool, deceive

例 他那么精明，想涮他可没那么容易。

► He is so clever. It's not that easy to fool him.

双规 shuāng guī

S

◆ double-designation

This term means a special investigation scheme of the Communist Party of China when a member or official of the Party is ordered to make an explanation of his/her alleged involvement in a discipline-violation or corruption case at a designated time and in a designated place.

例 他因涉嫌腐败案被"双规"了。

► He was selected for "double designation" for suspected corruption.

双开 shuāng kāi

◆ double expulsion; expel someone from the Party and from their administrative post as a punishment for corruption

例 昨天有一个高官因严重违纪被“双开”了。

► Yesterday, another high official was "double expelled" for severely violating the disciplines of the Party.

双赢 shuāng yíng

◆ win-win

例 一汽、丰田携手合作是一次真正获得“双赢”的决策。

► The cooperation between FAW and Toyota is really a great plan to achieve win-win goals.

爽 shuǎng

◆ 1. (of someone's nature) straightforward, frank, forthright, efficient; do something quickly

例 这人说话办事就是爽。

► This person speaks and does things efficiently.

◆ 2. to feel well, comfortable

例 他们总挑他的毛病，这让他很不爽。

► They always find fault with him, which makes him very uncomfortable.

S

顺 shùn

◆ 1. walk off with something, pick up something on the sly; shoplift, steal

例 他在超市顺了一瓶洗发水，让人给抓住了。

► He was caught shoplifting shampoo in a supermarket.

◆ 2. handy, convenient and easy to use; smoothly; without difficulty

例 等这条路修好了，到城里就更顺了。

► When the road is finished, it will be more convenient to go to town.

死定了 sǐ dìng le

◆ 1. be doomed to die or fail or lose

例 A：这一局比赛你是死定了。

► You are doomed to lose this game.

◆ 2. be doomed to be criticized or punished

例 B：你拿回扣的事儿被老板知道了，这回你死定了。

► You are doomed to be severely punished, for the boss already knows that you took the brokerage.

死扛 sǐ káng

◆ 1. go all out to support or shoulder responsibilities

例 这件事你尽管去做，有什么事我给你死扛。

► You do it (go for it). I'll shoulder the responsibility.

◆ 2. refuse to confess or reveal information

例 这事别人都告诉我了，你还死扛有什么用？

► Someone has already told me everything. What's the use for you to refuse to confess?

死性 sǐ xing

◆ stubborn, obstinate, inflexible, stiff; having a one-track mind

例 做事别那么死性,按照人家要求的去做就是了。

▶ Don't be so stubborn. Just do as they ask you.

素质 sù zhì

◆ quality (in manners), tact

例 这人真没素质,上车也不排队。

▶ This person has no tact and doesn't stand in the queue to get on the bus.

素质教育 sù zhì jiào yù

◆ education for all-round development

例 实施素质教育是中国提高国民素质、利于长远发展的需要。

▶ Carrying out education for all-round development is an important element in the improvement of national quality and in promoting the further development of China.

速配 sù pèi

◆ speed dating, flash love match, It refers to a matchmaking program or activity which helps the participants to find a boyfriend or girlfriend

例 在校园也搞速配恋爱活动,参加的同学来自同一院校的不同系。

▶ Speed-dating activities were also held on campus. Students who participated in the activities came from different departments of the same college.

S

塑身 sù shēn

◆ body shaping, shape one's figure

例 2007 年最热门的运动就是塑身运动。

▶ The most popular sport in 2007 is body shaping.

酸雨 suān yǔ

◆ acid rain

例 中国已成为仅次于欧洲和北美的第三大酸雨区。

▶ China has become the third largest acid rain region only next to Europe and North America.

随便 suí biàn

◆ as you wish, to suit oneself

例 A:你想吃点什么?

What would you like to eat?

例 B:随便,什么都行。

As you wish. Anything will do.

锁定 suǒ dìng

◆ 1. lock, stay tuned

例 锁定目标

▶ lock target

◆ 2. be interested in something, be in favor of

例 我就锁定这只股票了,等它一跌我就买。

▶ I'm interested in this stock and I'll buy it as soon as it drops.

T

抬杠 tái gàng

◆ quarrel, argue, bicker

例 他这是存心跟我抬杠。

► He is quarreling with me on purpose.

太有才了 tài yǒu cái le

◆ so talented, too talented; coming from a line of a famous Chinese short play

例 你真是太有才了！你怎么想出这个主意来的呢？

► You are so talented. How could you come up with this idea?

探班 tàn bān

◆ visit an actor or actress at the filming site

例 昨日来剧组探班的记者们，没想到却集体客串了一把群众演员。

► Journalists who visited the actors at the filming site yesterday didn't expect to become guest actors.

探底 tàn dǐ

◆ touch the bottom, down to the bottom

例 美股探底反弹。

► The American stock touched the bottom and rebounded.

陶吧 táo bā

◆ pottery bar

例 逛陶吧已成为新生代的休闲活动之一。

▶ Going to pottery bars has become a leisure activity of the younger generation.

套瓷 tào cí

◆ cotton up to; try to establish a relationship with someone; act as if one has a close relationship with someone else

例 他见到一个人就上去跟人家套瓷，也不管人家愿意不愿意。

▶ As soon as he sees someone, he goes to cotton up to them, and doesn't care if they like him or not.

套近乎 tào jìn hu

◆ try to get in favor with someone; try to create a close relationship with someone.

例 他有求于我，所以他才跟我套近乎。

▶ He wanted me to do something for him, so he tried to get in favor with me.

套牢 tào láo

T

◆ be tied up, consumed by

例 被股票套牢并不是什么怪事，谁都知道"股市有风险，入市需谨慎"这句话。

▶ It's not strange at all to be tied up by stocks. Everyone knows the phrase "The stock market is dangerous. Be careful if you enter into it."

踢皮球 tī pí qiú

◆ kick a ball; a metaphor for kicking something back and forth like a ball or passing the buck

例 政府部门遇事不再踢皮球，大大提高了办事效率。

► The government organs no longer kick balls when they encounter something difficult so they have greatly increased their working efficiency.

提速 tí sù

◆ raise speed, lift speed

例 自20世纪90年代以来，中国铁路经历了六次大提速，大幅度提高了旅客列车的运行速度，带来了巨大的经济效益和社会效益。

► Since the 1990s, China's railway has raised the speed of their trains six times. Increasing the speed of travelers' trains has brought huge economic and social benefits.

添堵 tiān dǔ

◆ increase someone's vexations; be upsetting, be a bother

例 见到她你可千万别提这伤心事，免得给她添堵。

► Don't ever mention this thing when seeing her, so as not to upset her.

T

添乱 tiān luàn

◆ increase the confusion or chaos; add to the trouble

例 你快走吧，别给我在这儿添乱，我都忙死了。

► You'd better go. Don't add to the trouble for me here.

调侃 tiáo kǎn

◆ joke, ridicule, scoff, mock, banter

例 他是一个幽默的人，喜欢调侃。

▶ He is a humorous person and good at banter.

挑染 tiǎo rǎn

◆ highlight, lowlight

例 发型设计师建议我把头发挑染一下，那样效果会更佳。

▶ The hair stylist suggested I highlight my hair for a more attractive effect.

跳槽 tiào cáo

◆ change jobs, switch job, job hopping

例 听说他跳槽去了一家外企。

▶ I heard that he switched his job to a foreign enterprise.

跳楼价 tiào lóu jià

◆ distress price, sale at breakdown price; It refers to selling something at an extremely low price.

例 几天前传出，家庭普通版的 Windows Vista 操作系统卖出跳楼价，从 1521 元降到 499 元。

▶ It was said a few days ago that Windows Vista family edition was sold at a breakdown price, from 1,521 yuan down to 499 yuan.

跳水 tiào shuǐ

◆ nose dive; a rapid fall in the stock market

例 沪市昨天在即将收市的10分钟之内,大盘突然跳水。

▶ In the Shanghai stock market yesterday, ten minutes before closing, stocks suddenly took a nose dive.

跳水价 tiào shuǐ jià

◆ cheap price, discount price

例 今年部分旅游景点的跳水价提前登场,这将有利于人们合理安排假期,早定出游计划。

▶ Discount prices for some tourist spots are provided ahead of time this year. It will be good for people to make an outing schedule earlier and arrange their holidays in advance.

铁杆儿 tiě gǎnr

◆ loyal

例 他是个铁杆儿球迷。

▶ He is a loyal football fan.

帖子 tiě zi

◆ 1. messages posted on BBS, mostly used in network

例 今天他发了不少帖子,有很多人跟贴。

▶ He posted (sent) many messages on BBS and a lot of people follow up with comments.

◆ 2. invitation card

例 他下周六结婚,现在正忙着给亲朋好友发帖子呢。

▶ He is going to be married next Saturday. Now he is busy sending invitation cards to his relatives and friends.

T

土 tǔ

◆ 1. unsophisticated, not well-informed, ignorant, inexperienced; a term used to describe someone who hasn't seen very much of the world

例 你可真老土,连这个都不知道,这是U盘。

► You are so ignorant and don't even know this is a U-disk.

◆ 2. uncouth old-fashioned

例 这件衣服太土了,穿上多难看呀!

► This clothes are too old-fashioned. How ugly they are!

脱贫致富 tuō pín zhì fù

◆ cast (shake, throw) off poverty and set out on a road to prosperity

例 将富饶的资源转化成财富是西部欠发达地区脱贫致富战略的特点。

► Turning rich resources into wealth is the characteristic of shaking off poverty and setting out on a road to prosperity in the less developed regions of China.

W

外出务工人员 wài chū wù gōng rén yuán

◆ migrant workers

例 这两年,随着外出务工人员的不断增多,人们的观念得到了彻底转变,从过去的"不愿出"、"不敢出"到现在的"争相外出"。

▶ In the past two years, as the number of migrant workers has increased, people's concept has completely changed, from "unwilling to go", or "dare not to go" to "striving to go".

外援 wài yuán

◆ 1.foreign player

例 本场比赛,申花队的四大外援都获得上场机会,并且都有不俗的表现。

▶ In this game, the four foreign players of Shenhua Team have all gained the chance to enter the court, and have made an outstanding show (performance).

◆ 2. foreign aid

例 这是赤峰市实施的第一个林业外援项目,项目总投资为 11370 万元人民币。

▶ This is the first foreign aid project of forestry implemented by Chifeng city, with a total investment of 113.7 million yuan.

外资银行 wài zī yín háng

◆ foreign bank

例 随着金融的国际化以及中国加入 WTO 后金融市场的逐步开放,外资银行大量抢滩国内市场。

► Along with financial internationalization and the opening of the financial market upon China's entering the WTO, foreign banks have swarmed to China to take advantage of the Chinese market.

完菜 wán cài

◆ over, finish with disappointing results

例 这件事看来要完菜。

► This thing seems to be over.

网吧 wǎng bā

◆ Internet bar

例 学校附近有很多网吧,晚上泡网吧的人可不少。

► There are a lot of Internet bars near the school. Many people stay in bars for a long time in the evening.

网虫 wǎng chóng

◆ web worm; a metaphor for Internet geek, Internet buff, or web fanatics

例 他是真正的网虫,除了一日三餐和睡觉,整天都泡在网上。

► He is a real web worm. He stays online all the time except for meals and sleeping.

网考 wǎng kǎo

◆ Internet-based test

例 2007 年底前中国托福网考将增加 14 次。

► By the end of 2007, use of the Internet-based TOEFL test will increase 14 times in China.

网恋 wǎng liàn

◆ online love affair, web dating, fall in love on web

例 经过一年的网恋，他们终于决定结婚了。

► After one year of web dating, they finally decided to get married at last.

网络暴民 wǎng luò bào mín

◆ network mob

例《纽约时报》等海外媒体将在网络发泄暴力情绪的部分网民冠以"网络暴民"称号。

► The *New York Times* and other overseas medias named netizens who give vent to their violent feelings on the Internet as "network mob".

网络空间 wǎng luò kōng jiān

◆ cyber space

例 人们呼吁反恶意软件、反流氓软件，净化网络空间。

► People request a fight against malware and rascal software to purify cyber space.

网民 wǎng mín

◆ netizen; net citizen

例 截止到 2006 年 6 月 30 日，我国网民人数已达到 1.23 亿。

► By the end of June 30, 2006, the number of China's netizens had reached 123 millions.

网校 wǎng xiào

◆ net school

例 如果让他上网校,他会变得更内向、忧郁、孤独。

► If you ask him to go to net schools, he will become more introverted, depressed and lonely.

网友 wǎng yǒu

◆ net friend

例 他是从一位网友那里得到这个消息的。

► He got this news from a net friend.

腕儿 wànr

◆ celebrity, famous person, expert, star; It mostly refers to famous actors and singers.

例 你不认识他? 他如今可是歌坛上一个不小的腕儿了。

► Don't you know him? He is a famous singer.

维和 wéi hé

◆ abbreviation for keeping peace

例 1. 有不少国家派出了自己的部队前去非洲维和。

► Many countries sent troops to Africa to keep peace.

例 2. 这是中国派出的第一支维和部队。

► This is the first peace-keeping troop sent by China.

维权 wéi quán

◆ abbreviation for defending rights, rights defense, rights protection

例 多年来农民工依法维权是一个社会高度关注的焦点问题。

▶ Rights protection issues for farm workers have been a highly concerned focus of society for years.

温室效应 wēn shì xiào yìng

◆ greenhouse effect

例 温室效应会使全球气温不断上升,它所造成的气候改变,将使我们付出巨大的代价。

▶ The greenhouse effect can make the global temperature rise and cause changes to the climate, which will cost us dearly.

文博会 wén bó huì

◆ abbreviation for International Cultural Industry Fair

例 文博会成为人们的节日,三天就吸引近了百万人次参与。

▶ The International Cultural Industry Fair has become people's festival. It has attracted nearly a million people to visit over three days.

例 厦门油画、漆线雕风靡中国文博会。

▶ The oil painting with lacquer thread carving (engraving) was displayed at China's Cultural Fair.

文化创意产业 wén huà chuàng yì chǎn yè

◆ cultural creativity industry, cultural and creative industry

例 目前我们正致力于通过文化创意产业,将精致的艺术文化融入我们的生活之中。

▶ At present, we're trying very hard to put refined art culture into our daily life through cultural creativity industry.

乌鸦嘴 wū yā zuǐ

◆ jinxing mouth, crow's mouth

Chinese believe the crow cawing could bring an unlucky spell on people. This term is metaphor for one who often speaks bad things or inauspicious words.

例 他是著名的"乌鸦嘴",提到谁,谁就会倒霉。

► He is well-known for a crow's mouth. No matter who he mentions, they will have a bad luck.

物权法 wù quán fǎ

◆ Property Law

例 中国《物权法》于 2007 年 10 月 1 日起正式施行。

► The Property Law of China was implemented Oct. 1 , 2007.

x

夕阳红 xī yáng hóng

◆ sunset glow, red setting sun, the glory of the sunset; It refers to happiness or joyful or glorious time of the elderly.

例 因为一首歌,"夕阳红"成了幸福晚年的代名词。

► Originating from a song, the phrase "sunset glow" has become a metaphor for the happiness of the elderly.

希望工程 xī wàng gōng chéng

◆ Hope Project; It refers to a project to enlist popular support to help children of poor families receive schooling

例 "希望工程"是一项社会公益事业,至今它已经走过了18年的历程。

► Hope Project is a social public welfare undertaking. It has endured a period of 18 years.

西部大开发 xī bù dà kāi fā

◆ development of the Western Regions (of China)

例 进一步推进西部大开发还将面临许多矛盾和问题。

► Further pushing forward the Development of the Western Regions will face many contradictions and problems.

嬉哈族 xī hā zú

◆ people who like hip-hop

例 他因为喜欢嘻哈音乐而成为嘻哈族一员,穿着打扮都是嘻哈风格。

► He likes hip-hop music and always dresses in a hip-hop style.

洗牌 xǐ pái

◆ riffle, shuffle; a metaphor for restructuring an industry

例 中级车市面临洗牌，一些想买车的人持币观望。

▶ The middle-level car market will face restructuring. Some would-be buyers are now waiting to see the results with money in hand.

瞎菜 xiā cài

◆ have no way out; be finished; be at the end of one's hope; be over

例 这活儿不能按时完成，咱们就瞎菜了。

▶ If this work is not finished on time, we'll be finished.

瞎咧咧 xiā liē lie

◆ make irresponsible remarks, speak groundlessly, talk nonsense

例 这件事还没谱呢，谁也不许给我到处瞎咧咧去。

▶ This thing has not been settled yet, so nobody should make irresponsible remarks to anyone.

下岗职工 xià gǎng zhí gōng

◆ laid-off workers

例 企业要妥善处理好下岗职工的生活问题。

▶ Enterprises should handle issues related to laid-off workers properly.

下网(线) xià wǎng (xiàn)

◆ offline

例 我要下网(线)了，有事给我发短信。

▶ I'm going to get off the Internet. Please send an e-mail if you have anything to say.

相当 xiāng dāng

◆ quite, fairly, rather

It comes from the lines of a famous Chinese short play.

例 这部新片可是相当的好看。赶紧去看,千万别错过机会。

▶ This new film is fairly good. See it soon and don't miss the chance.

香车美女 xiāng chē měi nǚ

◆ fragrant car and beautiful woman

例 一提到车展,人们就会想到香车美女。那些漂亮的新车和摩登车模最吸引眼球。

▶ As soon as a car exhibition is mentioned, people will think of fragrant cars and beautiful women. Those beautiful new cars and modern car models are the most eye-catching.

消费税 xiāo fèi shuì

◆ consumption tax

例 汽车消费税将进行调整,对低污染排放小汽车减征消费税。

▶ The car consumption tax will be adjusted. For low pollution emission small cars, the consumption tax will be reduced.

小贝 xiǎo bèi

◆ the nickmame for David Beckham

例 小贝热潮开始在美国升温。

▶ The heat for David Beckham began to rise in the USA.

小罗 xiǎo luó

◆ the nickmame for Ronaldinho Gaucho

例 小罗射失关键点球，球迷垂胸顿足。

► Ronaldinho failed in shooting a key penalty ball. The fans are so despressed at it.

小品 xiǎo pǐn

◆ short, simple literary or artistic creation, essay, skit, sketch

例 他演的小品最受大家的欢迎。

► The short skits he performed are the most popular.

小强 xiǎo qiáng

◆ nickname for cockroach

例 他的房间里时常有"小强"出没。

► His room was discovered to be infested with cockroaches.

小升初 xiǎo shēng chū

◆ students going from primary school to middle school

例 人们呼吁尽快建立一个小升初入学统一标准。

► People are calling for the establishment of an entrance examination standard for students going from primary school to middle school.

小资 xiǎo zī

◆ 1. Petty Bourgeois

This term became popular in the 1990s. It refers to people who long for western lifestyle and pursue spiritual and material enjoyment.

例 她是小资，每次过生日总要去吃西餐。

▶ She is Petty Bourgeois. Every time she celebrates her birthday, she goes to have Western food.

◆ 2. emotional appeal, taste, mood for life

例 她这人特别小资，对生活细节很讲究。

▶ She pays great attention to the appeal and details of life.

笑星 xiào xīng

◆ laughing star; It refers to well-known comedians or cross-talkers

例 为了让晚会更热闹，他们找来几个笑星活跃气氛。

▶ To make the atmosphere of the evening party more lively, they invited some laughing stars.

歇菜 xiē cài

◆ stop doing something, have a rest, stand aside

例 就你那两下子还想拿冠军？歇菜吧。

▶ You want to win the championship with your poor skills? You'd better have a rest. (You'd better forget it.)

邪 xié

◆ irregular, abnormal, strange

例 这两天邪了，一到早上六点他就醒，平常叫都叫不醒他。

▶ It's strange that he woke up at 6 a.m. these past two days. Usually nobody can wake him up.

邪门儿 xié ménr

◆ abnormal, weird, strange, odd

例 真是邪门儿,他只是个农民,怎么会有那么多人被他骗了呢?

▶ That's weird. He's only a farmer. How could so many people be cheated by him?

新新人类 xīn xīn rén lèi

◆ new generation; people born during the 1980s and 1990s

例 出生于20世纪八九十年代的新新人类在思维方式、情感表达方式和行为方式等方面标新立异,领先社会潮流,追求个性凸现。

▶ The new generation born in the 1980s and 1990s do things unconventionally in ways of thinking, emotional expressions and behavior. They also keep ahead of social trends, pursuing ways to display their own personalities.

信息高速路 xìn xī gāo sù lù

◆ information superhighway, digital superhighway

例 1. 各市积极铺就信息高速路。

▶ The information superhighways are under active construction in all cities.

例 电信、思科携手共建信息高速路。

▶ Telecom and Cisco joined hands to create the information superhighway.

信息化 xìn xī huà

X

◆ information-based, informationization

例 世界各国纷纷以信息化为基点进行产业结构调整和经济重组。

▶ Countries in the world have started industry restructuring and economic reform based on informationization.

形象大使 xíng xiàng dà shǐ

◆ Image ambassador

例 奥斯卡影后瑞茜·威瑟斯彭成为雅芳化妆品直销公司历史上首位全球形象大使。

► Reese Witherspoon, the Oscar queen, signed a contract with Avon and became the first Global Image Ambassadress in the history of the company.

形象工程 xíng xiàng gōng chéng

◆ Image improvement project, image-saving or face-saving project

例 他们正在美化城市，搞形象工程。

► They are beautifying the city and starting an image improvement project.

熊 xióng

◆ impotent, timid, faint-hearted

例 你真够熊的，他那么打你，你怎么都不敢还手？

► You are so timid. He beat you so heavily. Why didn't you strike back?

熊市 xióng shì

◆ bear market, (stock) market with falling prices

例 告别五年熊市，2006 年中国股市终于迎来"猛牛"。

► After five years' bear market, China's stock market finally met with the "vigorous bull" in 2006.

悬 xuán

◆ dangerous, precarious, perilous

例 真悬！这球差点就进去了。

▶ How precarious! That ball was almost kicked in(for a goal).

◆ almost impossible

例 A: 你觉得这件事能办成吗?

▶ Do you think it can be done?

B: 我看悬。

▶ I think it's almost impossible.

悬的乎 xuán de hū

◆ dangerous, perilous, unsafe

例 看你把这些碗放的地方,悬的乎的。

▶ Look where you put these bowls. It's so dangerous.

选秀 xuǎn xiù

◆ beauty contest show, talent show

例 电视上有不少选秀的节目,让人看得眼花缭乱。

▶ There are many talent programs on TV which offer people a dazzling show.

循环经济 xún huán jīng jì

◆ circular economy, cyclic economy

例 中国的循环经济,不是要建立一种简单的环境管理模式,而是在探索一种新的经济发展模式。

▶ China's cyclic economy is not in as a simple environmental administration mode, but rather is exploring new economic development.

y

亚健康 yà jiàn kāng

◆ sub health, sub-state of mental health

例 1. 随着社会生活节奏加快，在繁忙嘈杂的都市，亚健康人群越来越多。

▶ As the rhythm of life accelerates in busy and noisy cities, the number of people in sub health situations is continually growing.

例 2. 许多白领人士，由于工作极度繁忙，身体普遍处于亚健康状态。

▶ Because of high work pressure, many white collar workers are in the sub-state of mental health.

洋 yáng

◆ 1. foreign flavor, western style

例 这座楼房盖得够洋的。

▶ This building was built in the Western style.

◆ 2. foreign, outlandish, stylish

例 这个人穿着挺洋的。

▶ This person dresses very stylishly.

养犬 yǎng quǎn

◆ raise dogs; dog raising, dog breeding

例 如今养犬的人很多，由此引发了不少环境问题和邻里之间的矛盾。

▶ There are many people raising dogs today, which triggers many environmental problems and conflicts among neighbors.

养眼 yǎng yǎn

◆ pleasing to the eyes, eye pleasing, eye candy, visual enjoyment

例 他不得不承认，看美女的确很养眼。

► He has to admit that looking at beautiful women is really eye pleasing.

例 这的确是一部养眼的电影。

► This is an eye pleasing film indeed.

氧吧 yǎng bā

◆ oxygen bar (for oxygen therapy), fresh

例 白水寨方圆百里无工业污染，空气清新，负离子含量高，可谓是个天然大氧吧。

► Baishui Village has no industrial pollution within one hundred square kilometers. The air is fresh and the anion content is high. It's considered to be a natural oxygen bar.

幺蛾子 yāo é zi

◆ a crafty plot, a wicked idea or thing, a trick

例 他这人可不好对付，净给你整些幺蛾子出来。

► He is a person hard to deal with. He often plays wicked tricks on you.

摇头丸 yáo tóu wán

◆ ecstasy, a narcotic

例 他因涉嫌贩卖摇头丸而被拘留。

► He was taken into custody for selling ecstasy.

野蛮女友 yě mán nǚ yǒu

◆ wild girlfriend

This term originates from the title of a Korean movie, *My Sassy Girl*. It refers to girls who like to ill-treat or be barbaric to their boyfriends.

例 真不可思议，他这种性格人竟找了一个野蛮女友，而且还非常爱她。

▶ It's incredible. A person like him with such character found a wild girlfriend in the end and loves her very much.

夜猫子 yè māo zi

◆ night owl; a metaphor for a person who stays up late at night

例 他是个夜猫子，晚上不睡，白天不起。

▶ He is a night owl, who neither goes to sleep at night nor gets up in the morning.

一把手 yì bǎ shǒu

◆ 1. leading official in a unit, number one, first-in-command

例 他最近升为一把手了。

▶ He has recently been promoted to first-in-command.

◆ 2. good hand, able person

例 他可是翻译这行的一把手，找他翻这本书没问题。

▶ He is a good hand in the translation field. It's no problem to ask him to translate this book.

一步到位 yí bù dào wèi

◆ to reach one's goal in one step

例 他想一步到位，买个大房子。

▶ He wants to buy a big house so as to reach his residential

Y

goal in one step.

一卡通 yì kǎ tōng

◆ smart card, all-purpose card

例 他想办一张一卡通,乘车更方便。

▶ He wants to buy a smart card so as to take buses more conveniently.

伊妹儿 yī mèir

◆ e-mail

例 你有伊妹儿地址吗? 回头我把照片发给你。

▶ Have you got an e-mail address? I'll send those photos to you then.

以人为本 yǐ rén wéi běn

◆ people-oriented, people foremost, human-oriented

例 城市建设应处处体现以人为本的理念。

▶ City construction should reflect a people-oriented concept throughout.

异类 yì lèi

◆ 1. alien species, (of birds, animals, grass, trees, ghosts, etc.) different from humans

例 异类入侵

▶ invasion of alien species

◆ 2. alien; different from others; strange, odd

例 他在主持人中是个异类。

▶ He looks different from other hosts.

应急预案 yìng jí yù àn

◆ emergency planning, contingency plan

例 1. 中小学校组织学生春游必须做好应急预案。

► Spring outings organized by primary schools and middle schools must include an emergency plan.

例 2. 国家安全监管总局接到事故报告后,立即启动应急预案。

► The State Administration of Safety Control started emergency planning right away after receiving the report of an accident.

应试教育 yìng shì jiào yù

◆ exam-oriented education

例 基础教育领域的一场深刻的变革是由应试教育向素质教育的转变。

► One profound element of reform to China's elementary education is the transition from exam-oriented education to quality-oriented education.

影响市容 yǐng xiǎng shì róng

◆ affect (impair or harm) city image (looks), negatively affect the image of the city

例 一些影响市容的破旧房屋被限令拆除或整修。

► Some old and worn-out houses which negatively affected the city's image were ordered to be demolished (torn down) or renovated within a certain time.

优化重组 yōu huà chóng zǔ

◆ optimize and reorganize

例 这个集团将对业绩差的公司实施优化重组。

▶ This group will optimize and reorganize companies showing poor performance.

悠着点(儿) yōu zhe diǎn(r)

◆ take it easy

例 这活儿不是一两天就能干完的,所以别着急,悠着点。

▶ This work can not be finished in a couple of days, so don't worry and take it easy.

油 yóu

◆ oily, slick, glib

例 他油得很,跟他做生意你可得多长一个心眼儿。

▶ He is very slick. You've got to be more cautious in doing business with him.

油耗子 yóu hào zi

◆ 1. gas mouse; a metaphor for someone who steals gas from others' vehicles

例 他汽车里的油很快就没了,他怀疑小区里有油耗子偷油。

▶ The gas in his car is used up very quickly. He suspects that there are gas mice in his community.

◆ 2. illegal dealer in petrol and diesel oil

例 汽油短缺肥了油耗子。

▶ The shortage of gas makes gas mice rich.

游商 yóu shāng

◆ wandering dealer, one who doesn't have a booth to sell goods, but sells goods on the streets or anywhere he or she goes

例 工商管理部门对游商加大管理力度。

▶ Departments of administration for industry and commerce put more pressure on the administration to control wandering dealers.

有偿新闻 yǒu cháng xīn wén

◆ paid news

例 尽管有偿新闻被明文禁止,但却仍然频频出现在各大媒体中。

▶ Although paid news stories are proclaimed in writing to be forbidden, they still appear frequently in all kinds of media.

有门儿 yǒu ménr

◆ have a way out, be hopeful

例 1. 这件事你找他去办,准有门儿。

▶ If you ask him for help in this matter, it's hopeful.

例 2. 嘿,有门儿,你再跳高一点就够着了。

▶ Hey, don't give up. You can touch it if you jump a little higher.

有戏 yǒu xì

◆ hopeful, possible, likely

例 如果你去参加这个比赛,肯定有戏,起码能获得一块铜牌。

▶ If you go to take part in the competition, it's possible for you to win a bronze medal at least.

有氧运动 yǒu yǎng yùn dòng

◆ aerobic exercise

例 很多运动方式都属于有氧运动,比如:步行、爬山、划船、游泳等。

▶ Many sports in our lives may be considered aerobic exercise, such as walking, mountain climbing, boating, swimming and so on.

娱记 yú jì

◆ entertainment reporter; reporter who reports entertainment news

例 资深娱记批露了 39 位明星的生活隐私。

► The senior entertainment reporter revealed the private lives of 39 stars.

舆论导向 yú lùn dǎo xiàng

◆ direction of public opinion

例 各大媒体要加强正确的舆论导向。

► All media should encourage the right direction of public opinion.

郁闷 yù mèn

◆ bored, depressed; a phrase used by the young to express a fretful bad mood

例 真郁闷，打了 N 多电话也没找到他。

► How depressing! I made numerous phone calls but still couldn't find him.

原生态 yuán shēng tài

◆ original ecology; primitive

例 1. 原生态歌手

► primitive singer

例 2. 我们应该把建设人工绿地与保护原生态的自然绿地结合起来。

► We should combine building man-made greenbelts with protection of the natural greenbelt of the original ecology.

月光族 yuè guāng zú

◆ moonlight clan

It refers to people who spend all their salary (earnings) every month.

例 我儿子是典型的月光族,不管挣多少,到了月底一准儿花光。

► **My son is typical of the moonlight clan. No matter how much he earns, he spends all his money by the end of the month.**

晕 yūn

◆ no way out; incredible; out of expectation

例 A:小姐,别哭了。你的手伤我们能治好。

► **Miss, don't cry. We can cure your hand.**

B:我不是为手哭。而是我不知道手上的那块劳力士手表哪去了?

► **I'm not crying for my hand, but the Rolex watch on my hand. I don't know where it is.**

A:晕!

► **My God!**

晕菜 yūn cài

◆ feel dizzy, get confused, be muddleheaded

例 他没想到考试有这么难,光看了一下题目就晕菜了。

► **He didn't expect the exam to be so difficult. He felt dizzy by simply looking at the questions.**

Z

造势 zào shì

◆ create an atmosphere; promote

例 影片还未上映，各大报纸就已经纷纷开始为它造势了。

► The film has not yet been shown, but all the big newspapers have already started promoting it.

噪音污染 zào yīn wū rǎn

◆ noise pollution

例 噪音污染已经成为影响人们身体健康和生活质量的严重问题。

► The noise pollution has become a serious problem affecting people's health and quality of life.

增值服务 zēng zhí fú wù

◆ value-added service

例 购买这种产品，厂家将为用户提供增值服务。

► Customers who purchase this product will receive value-added service provided by the factory.

扎堆 zhā duī

◆ get together, gather around

例 中国人喜欢扎堆——扎堆聊天，扎堆购物、出游，就连结婚生孩子也扎堆。

▶ Chinese people like to get together to chat, go shopping and outing, even give birth.

摘牌 zhāi pái

◆ delist

例 这家公司因业绩不好被摘牌了。

▶ This company was delisted because of its bad performance.

涨停 zhǎng tíng

◆ harden, rise to become stable

例 农产品期货全面涨停。

▶ The futures of farm produce hardened in an all-round way.

朝阳行业 zhāo yáng háng yè

◆ sunrise industry

例 作为一个新型的、高速发展的朝阳行业，管理咨询业目前还存在很多问题。

▶ As a new and rapidly developing sunrise industry, management consulting has had many problems.

招商引资 zhāo shāng yǐn zī

◆ attract investment from overseas

例 他们不断加大招商引资力度，并在努力构筑招商引资平台方面取得了较好的成绩。

▶ Continuously putting more stress on attracting investment from overseas, they try hard to make better achievements in setting up platforms for attracting such investments.

找不着北 zhǎo bù zháo běi

◆ unable to find the direction North

It refers to getting confused; knocked out.

例 结婚让他们俩忙活得都找不着北了。

► They were knocked out from so busily preparing for the weedding.

找辙 zhǎo zhé

◆ 1. find an excuse, use a pretext

例 他实在不想参加这个会,于是就找辙给推掉了。

► He didn't want to come to this meeting, so he found an excuse not to attend.

◆ 2. find a solution, seek a way out

例 她的工作遇到了一点麻烦,她正想辙呢。

► She encountered some trouble at work. Now, she is seeking a way out.

真格的 zhēn gé de

◆ serious, real, true

例 老板说谁再迟到就扣钱。看样子这回他是动真格的了。

► The boss said no matter who was late again, he would reduce his pay. It seems he was serious this time.

整改 zhěng gǎi

◆ reform and consolidate

例 1. 这家企业马上就要进行整改。

► This enterprise will soon be reformed and consolidated.

例 2. 公司要我们尽快拿出一个整改措施(方案)。

▶ The company asked us to implement a reform and consolidation plan as soon as possible.

整合 zhěng hé

◆ Integrate, consolidate, unify, unite

例 整合资源

▶ integrate resources

知本家 zhī běn jiā

◆ knowledge capitalist

It refers to intellectuals who become rich by using new knowledge.

例 网络年代催生了无数的知本家。

▶ The network age has created numerous knowledge capitalists.

执政能力 zhí zhèng néng lì

◆ ruling or governing ability

例 提高党的执政能力

▶ improve the party's ruling ability

直销 zhí xiāo

◆ direct sale

例 直销法主要用以规范直销行为,加强对直销活动的监管,防止欺诈,保护消费者的合法权益和社会公共利益。

▶ The Direct Sale Law mainly regulates the conduct of direct sales, strengthens the administration of direct sale activities, prevents fraud and protects the legal rights of consumers and public interests of society.

治理整顿 zhì lǐ zhěng dùn

◆ improve the economic environment and rectify economic order

例 主管部门令这家公司停产，进行治理整顿。

▶ The department in charge ordered this company to suspend production to improve management and performance.

智商 zhì shāng

◆ intelligence quotient, I. Q.

例 你到底有没有智商，怎么会干出这种愚蠢的事来？

▶ Why did you do such a silly thing? Isn't your IQ better than that?

智障 zhì zhàng

◆ mentally handicapped

例 中国现有智障人士约 1182 万人。

▶ China currently has about 11.82 million mentally handicapped people.

中超 zhōng chāo

◆ abbreviation for The Chinese Football Association Super League (中国足球协会超级联赛), commonly known as Chinese Super League (中超联赛) or CSL

例 新浪网体育频道全面报道全国 15 支中超俱乐部球队动态。

▶ Sina Sports Channel is giving an overall report covering the 15 teams of the CSL Club.

钟点工 zhōng diǎn gōng

◆ hourly worker, usually referring to housekeepers who are paid by the hour, also called 小时工(xiǎo shí gōng)

例 他请了一个钟点工，每天给他做饭和打扫卫生。

▶ He employed an hourly worker to do the cooking and cleaning for him every day.

钟点养老 zhōng diǎn yǎng lǎo

◆ care-service for senior citizens charged on an hourly basis

例 京城"钟点养老"服务的兴起，让白天上班的子女放心，也使老人摆脱了寂寞。

▶ The emergence of the care-service for senior citizens charged on an hourly basis not only rids elders of their loneliness, but also relieves their working children from worry.

主打产品 zhǔ dǎ chǎn pǐn

◆ dominant product, main product

例 这家公司的主打产品是电冰箱。

▶ This company's main product is refrigerators.

主打歌 zhǔ dǎ gē

◆ key song, main song, theme song

例 这首歌是他新专辑里的主打歌。

▶ This song is the key song on his new album.

主旋律 zhǔ xuán lǜ

1. theme, principal melody

例 这首歌的主旋律非常好听，好记也好唱。

▶ The principal melody of this song is very good and easy to remember and sing.

2. theme, main idea, basic concept

例 这部电影讴歌了改革开放、勇于创新的时代主旋律。

▶ The theme of this film sings the praises of reform, cultural openness, and brave innovation.

注水 zhù shuǐ

◆ infuse water into something unreal, untrue; a metaphor for adding unreal things to something

例 在招聘过程中遇到"注水"的简历已是常事，尤其是学历造假。

▶ It's common during job interviews to find untrue resumes, especially those with false educational background information.

抓瞎 zhuā xiā

◆ find oneself at a loss; be in a rush and muddle

例 运动员如果平时不严格训练，比赛时准抓瞎。

▶ If athletes are not trained strictly on a regular schedule, they will find themselves at a loss in competition.

专卖店 zhuān mài diàn

◆ exclusive agency, franchised store

例 所有这个牌子的衣服他都是去专卖店买的，因为怕买到假货。

▶ All his brand name clothing was bought in franchised stores because he was afraid of buying counterfeit products.

转轨 zhuǎn guǐ

◆ change tracks, change (the existing structure, etc.)

例 从计划型经济向市场经济转轨

▶ change tracks from planned economy to market economy

转会 zhuǎn huì

◆ transfer to another club

例 贝克汉姆转会西班牙的事情终于尘埃落定。

▶ David Beckham's transfer to Spain is finally settled.

转基因 zhuǎn jī yīn

◆ transgenic

例 很多人担心转基因食品的安全性。

▶ Many people don't want to eat transgenic food.

转制 zhuǎn zhì

◆ system transformation

例 公有医院转制为民营医院作为一种全新的尝试,将在医疗大环境的发展中产生积极的作用。

▶ The system transformation from publicly-owned hospitals to privately-owned hospitals as a brand new trial will have an active effect on the development of the medical treatment environment.

装嫩 zhuāng nèn

◆ pretend to be childish, lovely or young

It refers to one who speaks, dresses, or acts like a young girl or boy.

例 这个女演员很会在镜头前装嫩,五十多岁了,却总是装出一副青春少女的样子,真让人受不了。

▶ This actress is good at acting childish. Though she is over 50 years old, she still acts like a little girl, which makes people very annoyed.

装洋蒜 zhuāng yáng suàn

◆ pretend

例 别在这儿装洋蒜了，大家都看得出来你没病。

▶ Don't pretend. Everyone can see that you are not sick.

撞大运 zhuàng dà yùn

◆ try one's luck, blind luck

例 买彩票绝对是撞大运，所以，不要把它当回事，只是玩玩罢了。

▶ Playing the lottery is based absolutely on blind luck. So don't take it seriously. You just play it for fun.

追尾 zhuī wěi

◆ bump into the rear of the car in front, tailgate

例 由于大雾天气，公路上发生了多起汽车追尾事故。

▶ Due to heavy fog, many tailgating accidents happened on the highway.

追星族 zhuī xīng zú

◆ movie fans, pop music fans, sports fans, groupie, star chaser

例 刘德华的北京演唱会引来无数追星族，现场气氛异常火暴。

▶ Liu Dehua's concert in Beijing has attracted a large number of groupies. The atmosphere of the scene was extremely hot.

准房奴 zhǔn fáng nú

◆ quasi-house slave, house slave-to-be; a term referring to someone working exceptionally hard to earn enough money to buy a house

例 2006 年的广州房市简直让"准房奴"们心力交瘁。

▶ The housing market of Guangzhou in 2006 really made "the house slaves-to-be" exhausted both mentally and physically.

准妈妈 zhǔn mā ma

◆ mother-to-be

例 企业抓住时机，推出了一系列针对准妈妈们的各种产品。

▶ Seizing this opportunity, the company introduced a series of products targeted at mothers-to-be.

自驾游 zì jià yóu

◆ self-drive trip; this term refers to people driving themselves to holiday or leisure destinations

例 自驾游给北京郊区带来巨大的经济效益。

▶ Self-drive trips have brought huge economic benefits to the suburbs of Beijing.

自主创新 zì zhǔ chuàng xīn

◆ Innovation, indigenous innovation

例 中小企业唯有实行自主创新，才能提高竞争力。

▶ Medium and small enterprises can not increase their competitive strength unless they practice indigenous innovation.

自主品牌 zì zhǔ pǐn pái

◆ self-owned brand

例 政府鼓励企业开发自主品牌。

▶ The government encourages enterprises to develop self-owned brands.

自助游 zì zhù yóu

◆ self-help trip, self-help travel; this term refers to people who plan their own trips rather than engaging the services of a travel agency.

例 "黄金周"期间,有不少人选择自助游去香港。

▶ During the Golden Week, many people chose to take a self-help trip to Hong Kong.

综合国力 zōng hé guó lì

◆ overall national strength, comprehensive national strength

例 提高综合国力

▶ increase comprehensive national strength

综合治理 zōng hé zhì lǐ

◆ comprehensive treatment or administration

例 加强社会治安综合治理,创造良好的社会秩序,让人民群众安居乐业,是全面建设小康社会的重要保证。

▶ Strengthening the comprehensive administration of public security, creating good social order and providing people with peaceful and contented living and working environments are important things to ensure the overall construction of a wealthy society.

走出去 zǒu chū qù

◆ "Going Abroad" Strategy

例 "走出去"战略是维护中国经济安全和可持续发展的重要战略,是中国面向 21 世纪的大战略。

▶ The "Going Abroad" Strategy is important for safeguarding national economic security and sustainable development, and is also a great strategy for China moving into the 21st century.

走人 zǒu rén

◆ go, leave

例 如果你不想在这儿干，就走人。

▶ If you don't want to work here, you can go.

足球流氓 zú qiú liú máng

◆ football hooligan

例 警察抓了一批在球场闹事的足球流氓。

▶ The police caught a group of football hooligans making trouble at the football field.

组合 zǔ hé

◆ combination, group

例 参加这次声乐比赛的选手中有六个多人组合。

▶ Among the participants in the vocal contest, there are six groups.

钻石王老五 zuàn shí wáng lǎo wǔ

◆ a very wealthy bachelor

例 他不仅外表俊朗，而且还是个极富魅力的钻石王老五。

▶ He is not only a handsome man, but also a charming and very wealthy bachelor.

Z

醉驾 zuì jià

◆ get drunk and drive; drive while drunk

例 许多人因醉驾而丧生。

▶ Many people have died as the result of driving while drunk.

做大做强 zuò dà zuò qiáng

◆ be big and strong

例 发展绿色食品是食品企业做大做强的必由之路。

▶ The development of green food is an essential strategy for the food enterprise to become big and strong.

做局 zuò jú

◆ make a trap, lay a trap

例 股市里有那么多特别聪明的人为股票价值做局。

▶ There are many extremely smart people in the stock market using stock values to lay a trap.

做人要厚道 zuò rén yào hòu dào

◆ be honest and kind; a phrase from a famous movie

例 你做事情不要太过分,做人要厚道些。这样,以后遇到困难时才会有人帮你。

▶ You shouldn't go too far in doing things. Be honest and kind. In this way, when you have difficulties, someone will help you.

做秀 zuò xiù

◆ show

例 湖南卫视善于做秀，“超级女生”节目成功后，催生了一大批的跟风者。

▶ **Hunan Star TV is good at developing shows. With to the popularity of its program *Super Girl*, many similar shows quickly followed.**

字母词

high

◆ excited; do something to one's heart's content, enjoy oneself to the full; pleasant sensation; delight

例 你听听这段音乐，肯定让你感觉特别 high。

► Listen to this piece of music. It must make you feel high.

F1

◆ formula 1 car race

例 这是迄今为止最棒的 F1 赛车游戏。

► This is the best F1 car raing game so far.

IC 卡 IC kǎ

◆ integrated circuit card

例 在 70 年代，随着科技的迅速发展，一种集成电路卡，简称 IC 卡出现了，人们又称它为智能卡。

► In the 1970s, along with the development of technology, an integrated circuit card appeared. It is called IC card for short, or smart card.

IN

◆ trendy, fashionable

例 如果你想做一个够 IN 的女人，你就不能不看这本杂志。

▶ If you want to be a fashionable woman, you must read this magazine.

IP 卡 IP kǎ

◆ internet phone card

例 目前，市场上各类电信卡大致有 IC 卡、IP 卡、充值卡、上网卡等类别。

▶ Recently, various telecom cards include IC cards, IP cards, prepaid phone cards, Internet cards and so on.

N 多

◆ a lot of, many times

例 这道数学题太难了，我都做了 N 多遍了，也没个结果。

▶ This math problem is too difficult. I can't work it out even after trying many times.

责任编辑：翟淑蓉
英文编辑：顾　珺
封面设计：古　手
印刷监制：佟汉冬

图书在版编目（CIP）数据

流行汉语／李淑娟主编.—北京：华语教学出版社，2007
（我的第一本中国读物；3938）
ISBN 978-7-80200-388-0

I. 流…　II.李…　III.汉语－对外汉语教学－自学参考资料 IV.H195.4

中国版本图书馆 CIP 数据核字（2007）第 172123 号

流行汉语

主编 李淑娟

*

© 华语教学出版社出版
（中国北京百万庄大街 24 号 邮政编码 100037）
电话：(86)10-68320585
传真：(86)10-68326333
网址：www.sinolingua.com.cn
电子信箱：hyjx@ sinolingua.com.cn
北京外文印刷厂印刷
中国国际图书贸易总公司海外发行
（中国北京车公庄西路 35 号）
北京邮政信箱第 399 号　邮政编码 100044
新华书店国内发行
2007 年（16 开）第一版
2008 年第一版第二次印刷
（汉英）
ISBN 978-7-80200-388-0
9-CE-3855P
定价：39.80 元